Emotional Survival

An Emotional Literacy Course for High School Students

Tina Rae

Lucky Duck is more than a publishing house and training agency. George Robinson and Barbara Maines founded the company in the 1980s when they worked together as a head and psychologist developing innovative strategies to support challenging students.

They have an international reputation for their work on bullying, self-esteem, emotional literacy and many other subjects of interest to the world of education.

George and Barbara have set up a regular news-spot on the website. Twice yearly these items will be printed as a newsletter. If you would like to go on the mailing list to receive this then please contact us:

e-mail newsletter@luckyduck.co.uk   website www.luckyduck.co.uk

ISBN 1 904 315 29 1

Published by Lucky Duck Publishing Ltd

www.luckyduck.co.uk

Commissioning Editor: George Robinson
Editorial team: Wendy Ogden, Mel Maines, Sarah Lynch
Designer: Helen Weller
Illustrators: Tina Rae

Printed by Antony Rowe Limited

Contents

How to use the CD-ROM

The CD-ROM contains a PDF file labelled 'Worksheets.pdf' which contains worksheets for each session in this resource. You will need Acrobat Reader version 3 or higher to view and print these pages.

The document is set up to print to A4 but you can enlarge the pages to A3 by increasing the output percentage at the point of printing using the page set-up settings for your printer.

To photocopy the worksheets directly from this book, set your photocopier to enlarge by 125% and align the edge of the page to be copied against the leading edge of the copier glass (usually indicated by an arrow).

Introduction and background

During recent years there appears to have been an increased demand for resources and materials that support parents or carers in the process of developing children's Emotional Literacy. This demand may be linked to the Government's agenda on social inclusion that aims to ensure that even the most difficult and socially unskilled people can be included within the school context. The main impetus for developing this programme is the research that highlights the importance of developing these skills (Apter 1997 and Baker 1998, Goleman 1996, Grant 1992 and Rudd 1998).

Many of the resources currently available focus primarily on developing Emotional Literacy by fostering children's ability to cope effectively with their emotions and behaviours in a range of contexts. Developing such skills clearly advantages children both in and out of the school context. As Jean Gross (2000) states, "Emotional literacy, or emotional intelligence, is actually a better predictor for lifelong achievement than is conventional IQ. A person's IQ predicts only a small part of lifelong success – ranging from 4%-20%. Emotional intelligence, on the other hand, predicts about 80% of a person's success in life."

The importance of promoting Emotional Literacy

McCarthy and Park (1998) suggest a rationale as to why emotional learning of this kind is important to every individual. They stress the following points:

- Understanding emotions is directly connected to both cognitive achievements and motivation to learn.
- Dealing effectively with emotions helps individuals to develop more positive relationships and provide a sense of mental or psychological wellbeing.
- Those adolescents who are 'emotionally developed' are deemed to be better able to live with or cope with difference. Moral views and value systems are shaped by both attitudes and feelings.
- The sense of purpose and meaning that individuals gain in their lives is derived in equal parts from both feelings and understanding.

Sharp (2001) also provides four reasons for promoting the Emotional Literacy of children, parents, carers, and those in the 'caring' professions. He suggests that human beings need to:

- recognise their emotions in order to be able to label or define them
- understand their emotions in order to become effective learners
- handle or manage their emotions in order to develop and sustain positive relationships
- appropriately express emotions in order to develop as 'rounded people' who are able to help themselves and, in turn, those around them.

The last point perhaps suggests a close relationship between Emotional Literacy and mental health.

For Park (1999) this becomes a significant factor in the drive to promote emotional literacy both in schools and in the wider context of the workplace and our social institutions and organisations. Such a drive would appear to be crucial in the light of the findings of the survey carried out by the Mental Health Foundation (The Big Picture, February 1999). This study focused primarily upon the promotion of children's and young people's mental health and stressed the following, "Mental health problems in children and young people will continue to increase unless there is a coherent and holistic programme implemented to develop the emotional and mental health of our children."

Emotionally literate children are less likely to experience mental health problems and, if they do develop them, are less likely to suffer long term. Emotionally literacy is derived from a combination of parents or carers, schools and wider social networks (Ibid.:15).

Emotionally literate or mentally healthy adults

If children's emotional literacy is closely related to their mental health then it would seem logical that the same relationship would exist for their, parents and carers. Also, the fact that emotional literacy appears to derive from a combination of parents, schools and wider social networks, would suggest that all have some responsibility for children's mental and emotional wellbeing. Daniel Goleman (1996) highlights the important role that parents play, in that, "Emotionally adept parents can do as much to help their children with each of the basics of emotional intelligence: learning to recognise, manage and harness their feelings, empathising and handling the feelings that arise in their relationships." (Goleman 1996 page 191.) However, emotionally literate parents are not the only significant adults who can impact positively upon children's social and emotional development. It is vital to acknowledge and reinforce important ways in which and schools can and do make a difference – for all children, whether they are deemed to be at a high or low point on the emotional literacy continuum. Rutter (1991) highlighted how schools can help children to effectively manage the stresses and difficulties encountered in their own lives: "It is not High School achievement that seems to make a difference, rather it is positive experiences of a kind that are pleasurable and rewarding and which help children to develop a sense of their own worth together with the confidence that they can cope with life's challenges and control what happens to them." (Rutter 1991 page 8.)

An eco-systemic approach and the promotion of Emotional Literacy

As Mosley and Tew (1999) suggest, theoretical origins of applying a systemic approach to human behaviour rests in the work of Ludwig Von Bertalanffy (1950, 1968) and Gregory Bateson (1972,1979) and in the clinical practice of family therapy such as Selvini-Palazzoni (1973), Minuchin (1974) and De Shazer (1982,1985). Applications of these approaches within the school context were later developed by Molnar and Lindquist (1989) and Cooper and Upton (1990, 1994).

These approaches rest upon the premise that humans:

- are socially dependent upon their social context or environment for their emotional and mental wellbeing
- do not have absolute autonomy in terms of behaviour, that is they are both influenced by and have the ability to influence their social networks and circles.

Consequently any change within their system or network will have some kind of effect upon the system as a whole. The dual nature of humans striving for both a personal identity and a sense of belonging to a group, generally results in people operating within a group context or system. The behaviours that result can therefore be seen as a product of interactions within the group.

Developing or promoting Emotional Literacy within the school environment or within the family context would consequently have implications for all these social systems due to the ways in which they evidently connect and interrelate. Small changes made in one relationship, one classroom or one staff room will, at some point, impact upon other parts of the system. In order for these changes to have positive outcomes, that is promote the emotional and mental health of all involved, it appears to be vital that schools begin to promote the core competences of emotional literacy in the knowledge that they are doing so within such an eco-systemic framework and therefore have a greater chance of achieving their objectives.

The emotional curriculum

It appears that psychologists and authors disagree to some extent as to what the effective competences are or should be. However, there does appear to be some overlap or consistency between the so-called competences as detailed by Salovey and Mayer (1990), Goleman (1996, 1998), Steiner (1997) and Higgs and Dulewicz (1999). These include:

- self-awareness
- management of relationships
- motivation
- empathy or inter-personal sensitivity
- social skills
- emotional interactivity, that is putting all the above together
- conscientiousness and integrity (the individual's ability to accept personal responsibility and accountability for his or her actions and decisions alongside being open and transparent in their dealings with others).

For Sharp (2001), the key to achieving in these competences initially lies in the individual's ability to develop a vision of themselves and who they want to be, that is the ideal self, and to then establish and work towards the necessary personal goals in order to achieve that end result. He states that self-esteem is the evaluation or perception of our self-image and that this needs to be built upon in order to avoid what Gillibrand and Mosley (1995) called 'the downward spiral of low self-esteem'. For Sharp, "If self-awareness is the foundation of Emotional Literacy then enhancing self-esteem lies at the heart of the nurturing process." (Sharp 2001 page 34.)

In order to raise self-esteem and self-awareness it would appear necessary to adopt a positive attitude and to take control of thoughts and feelings in order to use problems and difficulties as a springboard to deeper insight (John Kehoe 1997) and to use adversity as a springboard to change. Adopting this kind of solution focused approach perhaps reinforces the fact that optimism can be learnt and developed over time. Edward de Bono (1967) has certainly shown that there are strong links between optimism and thinking and creativity, that is even when there is evident proof that there is no solution available to a particular problem, a new definition of that problem can still lead to a solution. It would seem then, that in order to promote the teaching and modelling of these key skills, schools would have to initially ensure that both staff and pupils' self-esteem was nurtured and protected within an optimistic and solution focused organisation. This may well appear to be an extremely tall order on first glance, but remaining optimistic is essential and it is important not to lose sight of the fact that schools really do matter and can make a difference (Mortimore 1988, Rutter 1979, Reynolds and Cuttance 1992).

The positive classroom

Fostering and teaching the core competences of Emotional Literacy can therefore best be done within the framework of a positive classroom climate. Hey McBeer's (2000) work on teacher effectiveness shows that pupils would be more willing to try new things and to learn from their mistakes if they felt emotionally supported by their within teacher the classroom context. However, as Emotional Literacy also encompasses areas and systems outside of this context it is also essential that staff, parents or carers and pupils ensure that the core competences permeate and inform policy and practice in all curriculum and non-curriculum areas.

Strategies and techniques

There now exists a wealth of materials which are designed to promote the Emotional Literacy of children and adults alongside the wealth of research (mainly American) highlighting the benefits of becoming emotionally literate and developing the necessary social and emotional skills to modify and change behaviour (Greenberg and Kusch 1993, Elias and Clubby 1992).

Strategies and techniques developed in and used by schools include the following:

- PSHE programmes and resources (for example, lessons on feelings and managing feelings)
- Circle Time approaches
- working on methods of self-control
- drama or role-play or puppet work focused on feelings, relationships, problem-solving and self-management
- parenting skills programmes
- assemblies
- tutor time
- peer mediation and conflict resolution
- anger management groups and programmes
- social skills training
- assertiveness skills training
- problem-solving sessions using solution focused brief therapy techniques
- stress management groups or lessons
- self-esteem building groups, programmes and resources
- mentoring programmes or systems
- buddy support systems
- nurture groups
- Circle of Friends approaches
- transition projects (across key stages)
- counselling approaches.

Visit www.luckyduck.co.uk for resource materials.

This list is not designed to be exhaustive or to identify any research evidence as to the success of each type of approach. Rather it helps to highlight what many schools are currently doing in order to affect change at the individual, group and system levels. However, it does seem important to highlight some of these approaches and strategies for promoting Emotional Literacy as there is considerable evidence to suggest the success of specific strategies and techniques. For example, Peter Sharp (2001) describes how the use of anger management programmes and courses have aided in ensuring the inclusion and emotional development of pupils across a wide range of local education authorities (Faupel et al 1998, Johnson and Rae 1999, Sharp and Herrick 2000). Sharp suggests that the best local education authorities are those who do not only have such groups in place but also have a systematic plan to train, develop and empower the school staff to deliver this kind of emotional curriculum themselves.

There is perhaps more evidence from America and Canada to support the importance and value of promoting Emotional Literacy and to show the success of a range of programmes and resources in achieving this goal. Goleman (1996) is able to identify programmes which have been in place for over twenty years and have produced an improvement not only in the core competences of Emotional Literacy but also in terms of academic scores and performance. He has specifically described Steven Ash's 1987 series of friendship coaching sessions for so-called 'unpopular children' which appears to have had some degree of success. Ash coached the children to behave in ways that he perceived to be typical of more popular children. They were trained to talk with and ask questions of their partner in a game and to listen to and look at the other child in the game in order to see how they were doing or felt about things. They were also encouraged to 'say something nice' when the other child performed well and to smile and offer help, suggestions and encouragement as appropriate. Ash's sessions did not produce social stars according to Goleman but none were 'rejects'. Goleman also described Stone and Dillehunt's (1978) self-science curriculum which focuses upon the following components:

- self-awareness
- personal decision making
- managing feelings
- handling stress
- empathy
- communications
- self-disclosure
- insight
- self-acceptance
- personal responsibility
- assertiveness
- group dynamics
- conflict resolution.

It is perhaps the latter programme which has provided the inspiration to develop this book specifically for secondary school students. While it cannot in any sense be regarded as adopting an eco-systemic approach, it can hopefully go some way towards providing with a starting point to foster both the pupils' Emotional Literacy and their own skills and competences. Alongside this, it is hoped that through implementing such a programme staff will also become more aware of the need to re-evaluate and reflect upon their own emotional health alongside that of the people with whom they work and socialise with.

The structure of the programme

The programme is designed to be delivered to groups or whole classes of secondary school students either through extended tutor times or via the PSHE or citizenship curriculum. The programme is delivered in twenty sessions, each of which is designed to last approximately 45-55 minutes. However, each session can easily be delivered in shorter bursts and adapted to meet individual teacher's and student's requirements and the context.

Each of the sessions will generally include the following:

- An introduction to the emotion which briefly outlines the activities to be covered and provides a 'prompt quotation' to encourage the students to define the target feeling.
- An icebreaker activity to reduce stress levels and set the emotional tone of the session.
- Questions for Circle Time where the students will be given an opportunity to discuss times when they experienced this emotion.
- Activity sheets where the students can reinforce the concepts and ideas covered and further develop skills of self-reflection and self-awareness.
- The teaching of specific self-help strategies such as stress management, anger management and problem-solving skills as appropriate.
- The take home task for the students to complete in their own time which will also reinforce the concepts covered and the skills learnt.
- A plenary session in which the students can reflect on the session and what they have learnt.

Each of the sessions is designed to meet the following objectives:

- To enable the students to identify and gain a deeper understanding of the feelings they experience on a daily basis.
- To develop an emotional vocabulary.
- To further develop their ability to self-reflect, problem-solve and function within a solution focused framework.
- To further increase empathy for others and awareness of how personal feelings and behaviour can impact upon those around us.
- To develop a range of self-control strategies and to encourage the students to express anger and more difficult emotions appropriately, that is without resulting to physical violence or aggression.
- To encourage the students to develop and maintain their own personal motivation to change and succeed.
- To enable the students to become increasingly reflective and gain a greater understanding of consequences of both their own feelings and those of others.
- To enable the students to become increasingly aware of the links between feelings and behaviour.
- To improve the students' self-concept, confidence and self-esteem.
- To improve the students' social skills.
- To improve the students' ability to communicate effectively with others. To promote respect and tolerance.

Clearly these objectives can also formulate the success criteria for the programme. It is hoped that the students will be able to measure their own skills development in the core competences alongside being monitored and further assessed by a facilitator running the course.

How to use the programme

Each of the sessions is set out in a similar way to allow the facilitator to set up activities with ease. The following notes are intended to further clarify the purpose of each of the activities in the sessions alongside providing helpful hints. It is important to note that many of the resources such as the photocopiable sheets, the flip-chart and markers and chairs for Circle Time can be set up prior to the start of the session and are usually required in all of the twenty sessions.

Introduction

This introduces the specific feeling to be focused upon within the session and also usually aims at further clarifying the aims of the session and expected outcomes. The initial definition is intended merely as an introduction to the feeling and enables both the teacher and the students to identify the feeling and to label it for themselves. The definition given at the start of each session can be written onto the white board by the teacher prior to the start of the session. It is preferable to make use of the white board for this part of the session as this can be the focus of the initial whole-class brainstorming or discussion session. The brainstorming approach can be used to encourage the students to offer their own definitions and ideas with the teacher or a nominated student acting as a scribe. In this way a list of definitions can be produced and owned by all involved. It is important to encourage the students to develop their own personal definitions for the feelings as this aids understanding and clarifies meaning on a more personal and individual level. However, as with the Circle Time approaches, all ideas need to be volunteered, that is the students should be allowed to pass.

Icebreaker

These short activities are intended to break down barriers and create a positive climate for the remainder of the session. Many of the activities involve the students in small role-plays and co-operative skills games. The intention here is to build up the group ethos and climate alongside reinforcing positive self-esteem and reducing stress levels and anxiety. They are also intended to be fun and set a relaxed tone for the session.

Questions for Circle Time

The next part of the session makes use of the Circle Time approach in order to focus upon the specific feeling and to encourage the students to become self-reflective and analyse their own feelings and behaviours more effectively.

Circle Time approaches have long been developed and used in schools in order to further develop whole-school value systems alongside teaching the students appropriate behaviours and a positive sense of self-esteem (Bliss and Tetley 1993). "Circle Time can be not only a way to boost children's self-esteem, but also a means by which to facilitate the exploration of ideas and reflection on emotional and social experience." (Warden & Christie 1997.)

As Jenny Mosley (1993) states, "Circle Time holds self-esteem building to be an essential aim," and ensures that all the students feel valued in their personal contributions. This process enables the students to develop their confidence and to participate within the context of a safe, secure framework where their contributions are respected. This tends to result in building more positive self-esteem for individuals as well as developing a strong group identity and sense of belonging. Regular use of this kind of approach can enable the students to:

- build up new friendships and consolidate their existing ones
- create a sense of trust in each other
- create a sense of belonging to a group

- develop their self-esteem and self-confidence
- extend their social skills in speaking and listening
- develop a positive attitude and maintain motivation
- develop empathy for others and promote understanding
- develop positive behaviours and the ability to self-reflect and modify behaviours
- become more assertive
- increase the level of the students' Emotional Literacy and self-awareness.

Given that Circle Time is such a strong tool and a positive approach, each of the sessions within the programme makes use of questions for Circle Time in order to both introduce and consolidate the students' understanding of the feeling being presented. A good use of such an approach is central to setting a positive tone at the start of each of these sessions and building upon the fun and stress free mood hopefully provided by the icebreaker activities. Throughout this part of the session it is recommended that the students have access to chairs or cushions and that they should not be required to sit on the floor or on the carpet. The students should be afforded real respect and sitting on a chair (as adults do) will serve to reinforce this important and symbolic message.

The rules for Circle Time or questions for Circle Time need to be agreed and owned by all the students involved and should be reinforced at the beginning of each session. These rules are identified in the initial session and need to apply during all Circle Time activities or brainstorming activities and during the final plenary for each session when the students are asked to contribute their ideas and summarise the session or learning outcomes. Examples of such rules are listed below:

- everyone needs to listen to each other
- everyone needs to take turns
- everyone needs to respect each others' space and ideas
- everyone has the 'right to pass'
- everyone in the group needs to give ideas and solutions
- everyone needs to use their imagination
- everyone must be careful not to criticise others' ideas but to build upon them
- everyone should respect each other's privacy and need for silence.

At the outset, the course facilitator will have been able to identify the students who may have more difficulty than others in taking part in this kind of activity. It is obvious that such students will require sensitive and careful handling and possibly additional support in modelling of appropriate behaviours and social and emotional responses. It may also be helpful to arrange for one-to-one mentoring or support sessions as and when appropriate.

Activities (Handouts)

These sheets aim to generalise and reinforce the feeling introduced in the session. Many of the suggested activities also aim to promote co-operative working practices, listening skills and self-reflection. Some of the sheets can be completed independently whilst others require the students to work as a pair or in a group. This is organised in this way in order to achieve a balanced programme and to ensure that the students can develop both self-reflection skills and the ability to work co-operatively and effectively with others particularly in terms of developing joint problem-solving and analytical skills. It may be the case that there is not adequate time to complete all the suggested activities and it is clearly the facilitator's job to assess which are the most pertinent and worthwhile in terms of a particular group being targeted. The activity sheets can be presented in A4 folders or home-made project books in order to ensure that a special record is kept of each student's work during the course of the programme. This also allows for self-reflection and for the students to assess their own development of Emotional Literacy skills over time.

Take home task

The final activity sheet for each session is a take home task for the students to complete on an individual basis in the home context. Once again these activities aim to generalise and reinforce the feeling introduced in the session to particularly enable the students to develop their personal skills and ability to reflect upon and modify their own behaviours or attitudes and feeling states. It is often useful to encourage the students to feedback on these activities during the introduction to the subsequent session. However, it is advised that this is left to the teacher's or facilitator's discretion and whether or not the students themselves feel that this would be a useful activity.

Consequently, the subsequent session plans do not include an initial feedback time at the start of each session. If the facilitator wishes to include this feedback in each session, then it is suggested that this is done prior to introducing the 'new' feeling that is at the start of the introduction or at the start of the Questions for Circle Time section.

Plenary

The brainstorming approach can be used in order to elicit the students' views as to the usefulness of each session. Not only is this an opportunity to summarise the skills and concepts covered but it is also important to encourage the students to reflect upon the usefulness of the tasks and perhaps to begin to identify ways in which they might be able to further develop their own skills. It may be useful to formulate a list of key questions in order to prompt thinking and participation in this part of the session. These might include the following:

- What have we learnt about this particular feeling?
- What have we learnt about how we experience this feeling?
- What have we learnt about how others experience this feeling?
- Are there any new concepts we have learnt?
- Are there any new skills we have been able to identify?
- How will this session impact upon us now and in the future?

The above notes are intended merely as guidelines to the facilitator and are not intended to act as a straitjacket for the implementation of the programme. What is most important is that the facilitator remains vigilant, sensitive and above all authentic in his or her response to the students and their own ideas and feelings. Whatever feelings, problems and solutions arise in each of the sessions, it can be safely assumed that some level of genuine emotional and social learning will result and that all involved will have some fun.

More detailed facilitator's notes are presented at the start of each session plan and many of these not only describe each of the activities in more detail but also provide some hints and pointers as to when things may or may not require more sensitive handling.

A final point

It is important to point out that this particular programme (like many others) cannot provide any magic wand formula to solve all the social problems evident within and outside of the school context. However, as both a psychologist and a teacher I remain convinced that if the general concept of teaching children to become emotionally literate is seriously understood and consistently incorporated into the curriculum with the school as a whole, positive and measurable outcomes will and do result. It is hoped that this particular programme, albeit one of many small drops in the ocean, will begin to trigger such positive outcomes alongside encouraging facilitators to re-evaluate not only their own Emotional Literacy levels but those of the institutions within which they work and the emotional content of the curriculum that they develop and teach.

References

Apter, T. (1997) *The Confident Child*, New York, London, Norton

Asher, S. & Williams, G. (1987) *Helping Children Without Friends in Home and School Contexts in Children's Social Development:* Information for Parents and Teachers, Urbana and Champign, University of Illinois Press

Baker, R. (1998) *Here's Health Magazine*, March 20 -22

Bateson, G. (1979) *Mind and Nature: A Necessary Unity*, New York, Dutton

Bliss, T., Robinson, G., & Maines, B. (1995) *Developing Circle Time*, Bristol, Lucky Duck Publishing

Bliss, T. & Tetley, J. (1993) *Circle Time*, Bristol, Lucky Duck Publishing

Boulger, E. (2002) *Building on Social Skills*, Staffordshire, Nasen

Casey, J. (2002) *Getting it Right – A Behaviour Curriculum*, Bristol, Lucky Duck Publishing

Cooper, P. & Upton, G. (1990) *An Eco-systemic Approach to Emotional and Behavioural Difficulties in School*, Educational Psychology 10 (4), 301-19

Dann, J. (2001) *Emotional Intelligence in a Week* Oxford: Hodder & Stoughton

De Bono, E. (1967) *The 5 Day Course in Thinking*, Harmondsworth Middlesex, Penguin Books

De Shazer, S. (1982) *Patterns of Brief Family Therapy*, New York, Guildford Press

De Shazer, S. (1985) *Keys to Solutions in Brief Therapy*, New York, W. W. Norton

Elias, M. J. & Clabby, J. (1992) *Building Social Problem-solving Skills: Guidelines from a School Based programme*, San Francisco, Josey-Bass

Furman, B. & Ahola, T. (1992) *Solution Talk: Hosting Therapeutic Conversations*, New York, Norton

Gillibrand, E. & Mosely, J. (1995) *She Who Dares Wins (A Woman's guide to personal and professional success)*, London, Harper Collins

Goleman, D. (1998) *Working with Emotional Intelligence* London. Bloomsbury

Gourley, P. (1999) *Teaching Self Control in the Classroom – a Cognitive Behavioural Approach*, Bristol, Lucky Duck Publishing

Grant, W. T. (1992) *Consortium on the School Based Promotion of Social Competence, Drug and Alcohol Prevention Curriculum*, San Francisco, Josey-Bass

Greenberg, M.T. & Kusche, C.A. (1993) *Promoting Social and Emotional Development in Deaf children: the PATH Programme*, Seattle, University of California Press

Hanko, G. (1985) *Special Needs in Ordinary Classrooms*, Oxford, Basil Blackwell

Johnson, P. & Rae, T. (1999) *Crucial Skills: An anger management and Problem-solving Teaching Programme for High School the students*, Bristol, Lucky Duck Publishing

Kehoe, J. (1997) *Mind Power: Into the 21st Century*, Vancouver, BC Canada Zoetic Lazarus, R. S. (1982) Thoughts on the relations between Emotion and Cognition, *American Psychologist* 37, 1019-1024

Maines, B. & Robinson, G. (1998) *All for Alex - A Circle of Friends*, Bristol, Lucky Duck Publishing

McCarthy, K. & Park, J. (1998) *Learning by Heart: The Role of Emotional Education in Raising School Achievement*, London, Colouste Gulbenkian Foundation

Mental Health and Adolescents in Great Britain (2000) London, Stationery Office

Minuchin, S. (1974) *Families and Family Therapy* London, Tavistock

Molnar, A. & Lindquist, B. (1989) *Changing Problem Behaviour in Schools* San Francisco, Josey-Bass

Mortimore, P., Sammas, P., Russell, E., Lewis, D. & Stoll, L. (1988) *School Matters: The Junior Years*, London, Open Books

Mosley, J., & Tew, M. (1999) *Quality Circle Time in the Secondary School: A Handbook of Good Practice*, London, David Fulton Publishers

Park, J. (1999) (*Director of Antidote: The Campaign for Emotional Literacy*) Unpublished paper presented at South of England Psychology Services Conference December 1999

Rae, T. (1998) *Dealing with Feeling: An Emotional Literacy Curriculum*, Bristol, Lucky Duck Publishing

Rae, T. (2000) *Confidence, Assertiveness, Self-esteem: A Series of 12 Sessions for Secondary School the students*, Bristol, Lucky Duck Publishing

Rae, T. (2000) *Purr-fect Skills: A Social and Emotional Skills Programme for 5-8 year olds*, Bristol, Lucky Duck Publishing

Rae, T. (2001) *Strictly Stress: Effective Stress Management*, Bristol, Lucky Duck Publishing

Rae, T., & Robinson, G. (2002) *Keep Your Coooooool! Stress reducing strategies for Key Stage 2 & 3*, Bristol, Lucky Duck Publishing

Reynolds, D. & Cuttance, P. (eds) (1992) *School Effectiveness: Research, Policy and Practice*, London, Cassell

Rhodes, J. & Ajmal, Y. (1995) *Solution Focused Thinking in Schools Behaviour, Reading & Organisation*, London, B.T. Press

Rudd, B. (1998) *Talking is for Kids: Emotional Literacy for Infant School Children*, Bristol, Lucky Duck Publishing

Rutter, M. (1991) Pathways from children to adult life, *Pastoral Care in Education* Vol. 9. No. 3

Rutter, M., Mortimore, P., Ouston, J. & Maughan, B. (1979) *Fifteen Thousand Hours: Secondary Schools and their effects on Children* London, Open Books

Salovey, P. & Mayer, J.D. (1990) *Emotional Intelligence: Imagination, Cognition and Personality* 9 (3), 185

Selvini-Palazzoni, M. (1978) *Paradox and Counter Paradox*, New York, Jason Aronson

Sharp, P. & Herrick, E. (2000) *Promoting Emotional Literacy: Anger Management Groups in Clinical Counselling in schools*, ed. Barwick, N. (2000) London, Routledge

Sharp, P. (2001) *Nurturing Emotional Literacy: A Practical Guide for Parents and those in the Caring Professions*, London, David Fulton Publishers

Sheldon, B. (1995) *Cognitive Behavioural Therapy: Research, Practice and Philosophy*, London, Routledge

Stone, K.F. & Dillehunt, H.Q. (1978) *Self-Science: The Subject is Me*, Santa Monica, Goodyear Publishing Company

Van Lier, A. (1988) *The Classroom and the Language Learner*, London, Longman

Von Bertalanffy, L. (1969) *General System Theory: Foundations, Development, Applications*, New York, George Brazillier

Wardle, C. & Rae, T. (2002) *School Survival: Helping students survive and succeed in Secondary School*, Bristol, Lucky Duck Publishing

Warden, D. & Christie, D. (1997) *Teaching Social Behaviour*, London, David Fulton Publishers

White M. (1999) *Picture This: Guided Imagery for Circle Time*, Bristol, Lucky Duck Publishing

Introductory Session

Introduction

In this initial session it will be important for the facilitator to clarify the aims of the project as a whole alongside introducing the purpose of this first session. As this is the first session in the programme, it does not follow the usual structure of subsequent sessions.

The facilitator can initially focus upon Activity 1 which includes two definitions of Emotional Literacy and also clarifies the key skills of Emotional Literacy which are due to be focused upon in the coming sessions. It may be helpful to write these two definitions on a whiteboard and to discuss them with the students at the outset alongside discussing the key skills of Emotional Literacy as follows:

- awareness of your feelings
- personal insight
- self-assurance
- self-regulation
- authenticity
- accountability
- flexibility
- self-motivation.

It will be important to stress that the aim of the course as a whole is to ensure that each participant can further develop each of these key skills.

Icebreaker

At the start of each session there will be an icebreaker activity which is intended to break down barriers and create a positive climate for the remainder of the session. This will usually then be followed by questions for Circle Time. It will be important to make the students aware of this structure and the fact that this will generally be consistent throughout the sessions. This first icebreaker can be linked to the questions for Circle Time. The icebreaker is entitled 'Emotional Telepathy'. For approximately one and a half minutes the students can sit in silence facing a partner. During this time they will not be allowed to talk but simply to look and to 'feel' in an attempt to 'pass the emotion over' to each other that they are feeling at that particular moment in time. Once the time is up, each student can feedback to the other as to what they think the other person was feeling. Were they right? Was it easy to read how someone else feels? Was there any moment when they began to feel what the other person was feeling?

Questions for Circle Time

The next part of this introductory session makes use of the Circle Time approach in order to focus upon the aims and objectives of the course as a whole. The students can be asked to consider the following questions:

How well can you recognise what others are feeling?
How well can you understand your own feelings?
How well do you express your feelings or manage 'difficult' emotions?
What do you feel the main purpose of doing a course like this is?
What do you hope to get out of the course?

(Clearly it will have been important to initially identify rules for Circle Time or group rules as discussed in the introduction to the course. It may be helpful to make use of our group rules sheet in order to record group rules at the start of this short Circle Time session. The sheet can be found at the end of this session).

Activity 1 – Definitions: Emotional Literacy

The students can discuss the key skills of Emotional Literacy as recorded on the handout of the same title and work with a partner in order to formulate their own definition for each key skill. It may be helpful to utilise dictionaries or thesaurus' in order to further formulate appropriate definitions. The students can record their ideas on the reverse of this sheet or on a separate piece of paper and then feedback to the group as a whole. What kind of agreements can they reach? It may also be helpful for the facilitator to record the students' ideas on a whiteboard or flip-chart and to pool their ideas in order to come up with agreed definitions from the group as a whole.

Activity 2 – How are your skills?

This is an individual activity in which the students can assess their skills in each of the key competences of Emotional Literacy as identified on the Emotional Literacy handout. This activity utilises a scaling approach and the students are required to read each of the statements and then tick against each scale, rating themselves 0 – 5 as to whether they feel they have or have not developed the skill listed. It is important that students recognise this is an initial rating. Everyone will probably be able to identify areas for future development and it would be extremely rare for a single individual to be able to rate themselves highly on each of the key skills. In practice, it may be helpful for the facilitator to participate in this activity and encourage the students to perceive the facilitator as being involved in this learning process in terms of developing their own Emotional Literacy. On completion of the personal rating scale, the students are required to identify their highest and lowest scores, their best skills and weakest skills, alongside identifying three things that they might do in order to improve.

Take home task – My personal target sheet

This self-assessment leads neatly into the next activity which encourages the students to record their personal targets onto an individualised target sheet. A scaling activity is used in order to prompt the students to record how positive they currently feel about themselves in their situation and about their current level of Emotional Literacy. This target sheet encourages the students to identify and articulate personal targets for future development alongside identifying the types of resources and other people in their lives who may be able to help them reach their goal.

Plenary

The circle or brainstorming approach can finally be used in order to elicit the students' views as to how they feel this session has gone and also to briefly summarise the main points covered and reinforce the main aims of the course as a whole. It may be helpful to use the following questions as prompts:

What have we learnt about Emotional Literacy?
How do we feel about this concept?
Is there any new language that we have been exposed to?
Have we been able to identify skills that we may need to develop?
Have we been able to identify skills that we already have?
What do we hope to gain from this course?
How do we feel this course will make a difference to us?

Definitions

Emotional Literacy

Recognising, understanding, appropriately expressing and effectively managing emotions in ourselves and in relationships with others.

People who are emotionally literate are able to get on with others, resolve conflicts, motivate themselves and achieve in life.

Key skills of Emotional Literacy

- awareness of your feelings
- self-assurance
- authenticity
- flexibility
- personal insight
- self-regulation
- accountability
- self-motivation.

Work with a partner and try and formulate your own definition for each key skill use a dictionary or thesaurus. Record your ideas on a separate sheet.

How are your skills?

How is your Emotional Literacy?

How do you rate? Read each statement and tick against each scale:

0 = not at all 3 = sometimes 5 = always

Awareness of your feelings	0	1	2	3	4	5
You know what you are feeling						
You can label your feelings						
You know when your feelings affect your work						
You know when your feelings affect your relationships						

Personal insight	0	1	2	3	4	5
You know your strengths						
You know your weaknesses						
You can take constructive criticism or feedback from others						
You don't take yourself too seriously						
You know when you've done something well and can feel good about yourself						

Self assurance	0	1	2	3	4	5
You act confidently in most situations						
You stick up for things you think are right						
Other people think you are confident						

Self regulation or control	0	1	2	3	4	5
You can stop yourself when you know you're behaving in a way that will cause problems (for you and others)						
You can keep calm under pressure						
You can handle uncomfortable feelings and use strategies to reduce stress and anxiety						

Authenticity	0	1	2	3	4	5
When you say you'll do something you do it						
You don't say or act one thing and then do another						
You can admit your mistakes						
You can stand up for what you think even if you are in the minority						

Accountability	0	1	2	3	4	5
You can take responsibility for your behaviour and actions						
You keep your promises						
You admit it when you've made a mistake						

Flexibility	0	1	2	3	4	5
You can cope with changes to your day						
You don't get stressed by change and can go with the flow						
You like to be creative and think of new ways of doing things						

Self-motivation	0	1	2	3	4	5
You like to achieve your best						
You like to get things done						
You are committed to your relationships						
You'll keep going even if things get tough						
You are optimistic and look for opportunities before you look for problems						

Stop and Think

What are your highest scores?
Where are your lowest scores?
Which is your best key skill and which is your weakest?
Try to think of three things that you could do in order to improve your skills:

1) ____________________

2) ____________________

3) ____________________

Take home task

My personal target sheet

Name ______________________________ Date ____________________

On a scale of 1 – 10, where I am now in terms of how positive I feel about myself and my level of Emotional Literacy:

(1 = very negative 5 = okay 10 = brilliant)

1 2 3 4 5 6 7 8 9 10

Where would I like to be on the scale?

In order to get there my targets will be:

1. ____
2. ____
3. ____
4. ____

Who can help me achieve these targets and how?

____

How can they help me?

____

How can I help myself?

____

When will I know that I've reached my goals?

____

What will be different?

____

How will I feel?

____

Now GO FOR IT!

Our Group Rules

RespectSupportListenConfidentialityEncourageRespect

The do's and don'ts of being on the Emotional Survival Course

We all agree to abide by our rules:

- ____________________
- ____________________
- ____________________
- ____________________
- ____________________

Signed ____________________ Date __________

RespectSupportListenConfidentialityEncourageResp

Session 2

Fabulous Feelings

Introduction

The facilitator can outline the main aims of this session and briefly describe the subsequent activities and tasks. The main focus is to encourage the students to develop their emotional vocabulary and awareness of the range and nature of the feelings that they experience on a daily basis. There is also an opportunity for the students to distinguish between comfortable and uncomfortable feelings and feelings which may be described as both uncomfortable and comfortable. The students are also required to consider a range of situations and to think about how they may or may not feel in each of these contexts. The final take home activity encourages the students to maintain a personal feelings diary and to attempt to identify further the connection between feelings and behaviour.

Icebreaker

This icebreaker is intended to encourage the students to read social cues. The students can play the game, 'In the manner of the word'. The students are required to walk into the room as if they were happy, excited, dejected, fearful, upset, lonely, scared or furious. The facilitator will have identified a student, asked them to remove themselves and provided them with a small card on which the feeling will be recorded. The student will then be required to either walk into the room or clean their teeth or go and sit at their desk in the manner of this word and the other students will be required to guess the emotion from looking at the student's body language, facial expression and so on.

Questions at Circle Time

Once the circle has been arranged the students can focus upon the following questions:

What feelings do we have?
What feelings do we usually experience when we wake up in the morning?
What feelings do we experience during the course of a school day?
What is the most comfortable feeling you have ever experienced and why?
What is the most uncomfortable feeling you have ever experienced and why?

Activity 1 – Brainstorm

This brainstorming activity encourages the students to identify how many feelings they have either experienced or are aware of currently. The questions at Circle Time may have helped prompt thinking at this point alongside encouraging the students to distinguish between feelings.

Activity 2 – Sort them!

This recording format allows the students to sort their feelings into three groups:

1. uncomfortable feelings
2. comfortable feelings
3. feelings which could be both uncomfortable and comfortable simultaneously.

They can begin to reflect more fully on their own feelings and the factors that may or may not have influenced these. The students are required to identify a time when they experienced mainly comfortable feelings and then to try and identify three factors which may have influenced them at this time. They are then asked to do this for a time when they experienced mainly uncomfortable feelings and a time when they simultaneously felt a mixture of both kinds of feelings. There is then an opportunity for the students to discuss these three experiences with a partner and to identify any similarities or differences in their own experiences.

Activity 3 – Situation cards

The facilitator will benefit from having photocopied these cards and laminating them prior to the session but if there is not time to do this then the handouts can simply be given to the students. The students can work in small groups and discuss each of the situations identifying how they would feel if they were put in this particular situation and how they may or may not respond. It will be important to emphasise that there may well not be a 'right answer or response'. The students may need to consider whether or not they agree with each other's views and the reason for any disagreement or difference of opinion. It will be important for them to consider the question, "Do we all feel the same in each of these situations or do we respond differently. If so why?" It may be helpful for each of the small groups to feedback to the group as a whole once the activity has been completed to everyone's satisfaction.

Take home task – a personal diary

This take home task requires the students to maintain a personal diary for a week. They are asked to record how they felt on each day and the reasons for their feelings. They can record how they were prompted to behave once they had experienced this particular feeling and what the consequences of their behaviour was. In this way, the students will be encouraged to consider further the link between their feelings and behaviours and how there may or may not be times when they need to manage their feelings more effectively in order to pre-empt or avoid negative behaviours which do not achieve the best possible outcomes.

Plenary

The circle or brainstorming approach can be used in order to consider the following questions:

What have we learnt about our feelings?
What have we learnt about the link between our behaviours and our feelings?
What have we learnt about other's feelings?
Are there any new concepts we have learnt?
Are there any new skills we have been able to identify?
How will this session impact upon us now and in the future?

Brainstorm!

Sort Them!

Using the feelings from the 'How many feelings do you have' activity, sort them into categories:

Comfortable feelings	Uncomfortable feelings	Feelings that can be both

Think of a time when you experienced mainly comfortable feelings and try to identify three factors that influenced your state:

1. ____________ 2. ____________ 3. ____________

Think of a time when you experienced mainly uncomfortable feelings and try to identify three factors that influenced your state:

1. ____________ 2 ____________ 3. ____________

Think of a time when you simultaneously felt a mixture of both uncomfortable and comfortable feelings and try to identify three factors that influenced your state:

1. ____________ 2. ____________ 3. ____________

Discuss these three experiences with a partner. Can you identify any similarities and differences in your experiences?

Situation Cards

How would you feel in each of these situations? Work in small groups and brainstorm your ideas. Do you agree with each other's views? Do we all feel the same or do we respond differently?

It is 9.00pm. You are walking home from your friend's house and someone is following you. How do you feel?	You are the only person in your form who cannot go on the Outward Bound trip as your Mum can't afford to pay. How do you feel?
Your maths teacher has accused you of cheating in a test and you know that you didn't. How do you feel?	Your best friend has recently put on a lot of weight and is feeling down about herself. She doesn't want to go out or have anything to do with you. How do you feel?
Your elder brother has joined a gang and you know that they are all into soft drugs and shoplifting. He says it's none of your business. How do you feel?	Your Mum has got a new boyfriend. He continually moans at you for not being tidy around the house and says you're lazy. How do you feel?
Your gran died last week. You were really close to her and used to go shopping every Saturday. How do you feel?	You have just found out that your sister has won a million pounds on the lottery. How do you feel?
Your Dad has just left home and gone to live with his girlfriend leaving you and your sister to live with your Mum. How do you feel?	The exams start next week and you know that you haven't done enough revision. How do you feel?

Situation Cards

The bus is late and you are standing in the rain watching a gang of boys yelling and laughing as they walk towards you. How do you feel?	Your little brother is being bullied by three boys in your year group. How do you feel?
You overhear your friends talking about you and they are saying that you are a bit mean and selfish. How do you feel?	You worked really hard on your History project and made sure it was beautifully presented. The teacher said it was a scrappy piece of work. How do you feel?
You have won an award for the 'best effort' in English. How do you feel?	Last week there was an arson attack and the IT unit at school was burnt down. You know who did it. How do you feel?
You find reading and writing really difficult and can't always manage to write down the homework tasks in your Link book. How do you feel?	At your friend's party last Friday, the person that you really liked went off with someone else and seemed to ignore you. How do you feel?

Take Home Task

A Personal Diary

Try to keep this feelings diary for one week. Record how you felt each day and the reasons for feeling this way. Then record how you behaved and what happened next – the consequences!

	Why I felt like this	How did I behave or what did I do?	What happened next
Sunday feelings			
•			
•			
•			
Monday feelings			
•			
•			
•			
Tuesday feelings			
•			
•			
•			
Wednesday feelings			
•			
•			
•			
Thursday feelings			
•			
•			
•			
Friday feelings			
•			
•			
•			
Saturday feelings			
•			
•			
•			

Session 3

Feeling Accepted

Introduction

The facilitator can initially clarify the aims and outline the content of this session. The students will be able to consider the feeling of acceptance and to identify when they do and do not experience such a feeling. They will also be asked to further build upon their own self-esteem and feeling of acceptance within their peer group. The notion of positive self-acceptance and the importance of valuing and accepting yourself will also be focused upon. The students will be encouraged to consider the importance of self-acceptance and the way in which this may impact upon how much they, themselves, accept and like others. Then students will finally be encouraged to identify areas for further future development.

The facilitator may wish to write up an initial prompt or definition on the whiteboard in order to trigger the students' thinking and clarify the feeling to be focused upon in this session. This might look as follows:

Feeling accepted is when you know that people like you or love you for who you are and not for who you might be.

Icebreaker

This icebreaker is entitled 'Increase Your Word Power'. This particular activity focuses upon further building the students' ability to articulate their own feelings and to recognise the importance for further developing an emotional vocabulary. The facilitator can write three words on the whiteboard as follows:

1. OK
2. Gutted
3. Cool.

These are considered to be the three main ways in which so-called 'teenagers' respond when asked the question, "How do you feel?" The students are then asked the following question:

How many other words can you find to describe these three?

They can work in groups of four and then feedback to the group as a whole.

Questions for Circle Time

During this part of the session the students can focus upon the following questions:

What does feeling accepted actually mean?
How have we experienced this feeling?
When have we not felt accepted?
When people don't feel accepted, what do we think happens to their behaviour?
How can we show others that we accept and like them?
Why is it important to accept and like ourselves?

Activity 1 – Circles of acceptance

This activity requires the students to complete the Circles of Acceptance by identifying the people who they know who make them feel accepted. Initially they are asked to identify parents, carers or siblings and then friends or special people in their lives. The final circle requires them to identify people who may be paid to look after them or to include them within their lives, support them in their learning and so on. The students are then asked to identify three people from the chart and record what they think they do in order to make them feel accepted. This encourages the students to think carefully about how others may or may not perceive them and to further distinguish between feelings, words and actions.

Activity 2 – Acceptance cards

This acceptance game requires the students to work in a group of six to eight. The students are given the second handout which can be photocopied on to card so that they are able to quickly cut out each of the acceptance cards. One student is then nominated to shuffle these cards and to take the top card, completing the sentence or answering the question written on it. The card is then returned to the bottom of the pile and the game continues around the group. The students can take an alternative card or pass if they feel unable to cope with the question or request. The main idea here is to encourage the students to identify positive points about themselves alongside articulating positive feelings that they have about others and that others may have about them. This activity also encourages the students to recognise the importance of accepting and supporting each other and developing the ability to be honest and supportive without criticising others or doing them down in any way.

Activity 3 – Blow your own trumpet

This individual activity requires the students to identify their talents and achievements. It reinforces the importance of accepting and valuing oneself. Feeling positive, motivated and accepted allows you to be able to respond confidently to others and ensure that they feel respected and valued by you.

It is up to the facilitator (and possibly the available time) as to whether or not the students can complete this activity for a friend. However, it's probably a good idea to have additional copies of the handout available – just in case.

Take home task – self-assessment quiz

This encourages the students to again utilise a scaling technique in order to identify the extent to which they currently accept and like themselves. The students are asked to rate themselves against a series of statements, for example I feel happy, I am confident, I try hard, I feel adventurous, I am kind, I am sensitive. The second part of the assessment requires them to then identify the five qualities and feelings that they rated the highest and their lowest ratings and to then articulate a preferred future rating. They are then required to consider how they may achieve such preferred future ratings by identifying the following:

- things they can do to help themselves
- things others can do to help them
- things that can be changed around them which may help them further
- what would be different if they actually were able to reach this preferred future?

Plenary

The circle or brainstorming approach can be used in order to address the following questions:

What have we learnt about this particular feeling?
What have we learnt about how we experience this feeling?
Have we learnt about how others experience this feeling?
Are there any new concepts or language that we have learnt?
Are there any new skills that we have been able to identify?
How will this session impact upon us now and in the future?

Circles of Acceptance

Feeling Necessary

Complete the Circles of Acceptance by writing in the names of all the people you know who make you feel accepted.

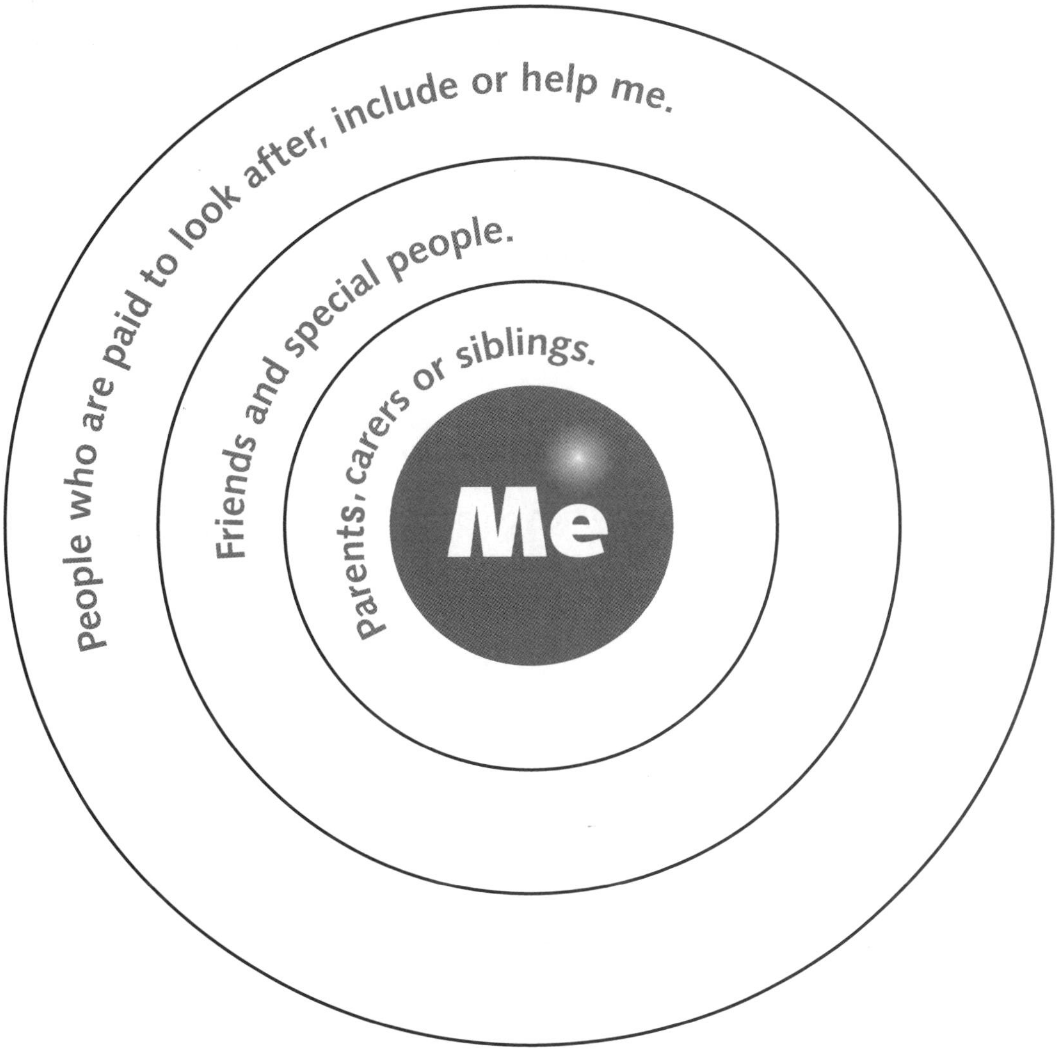

Identify three people from the chart. Record what they think, say and do in order to make you feel accepted.

Person 1 thinks ______________ says ______________ does ______________

Person 2 thinks ______________ says ______________ does ______________

Person 3 think ______________ says ______________ does ______________

Acceptance Cards

It's Good to be You!

Cut out the cards and play the Acceptance Game! Work in a group of 6-8 and nominate one person to shuffle the cards and take the top card, completing the sentence or answering the question. Return the card to the bottom of the pile and continue around the group. The students can take another card or pass if necessary. Enjoy the game! (The two sheets provide 30 cards for each group.)

I'm good at...	To person opposite – say two things that you like about them.	I know I'm successful when...
I'm getting better at...	I know when others accept me because...	My best point is...
My main strengths are...	My Mum or Dad or carer thinks I'm good at...	My best day was ...
I think my friends like me because...	I know that my Mum or Dad or carer accept me for who I am because...	My friends like me because...
I like myself because...	I feel positive when...	My best subject is...

Acceptance Cards

I care a lot about...	If you could be anyone else in the group who would it be and why?	The best bit about how I look is...
What is most important to me is...	It's Good to be You!	My greatest talent is...
I feel important when...	To person opposite – what do people like about him or her?	I know I have the power to...
My best achievement is...	In this game I most respect because...	My best quality is...
to person on your right – identify two positive things about them.	I feel confident when...	to person on your left – identify two positive things about them.

Blow Your Own Trumpet

I accept and value myself because...

I'm talented!

I am good at:

1. ______

2. ______

3. ______

I look OK!

My good features are:

1. ______

2. ______

3. ______

I'm accepted and liked!

I am good at:

1. ______

2. ______

3. ______

I'm a quality person!

My best qualities are:

1. ______

2. ______

3. ______

I can do it!

My achievements include:

1. ______

2. ______

3. ______

Turn it around!

Could you fill in this sheet for a friend and show them that you accept and respect them? Ask for another photocopy of the sheet and have a go!

Remember! Accepting and valuing yourself and others generally achieves the best outcome all round!

Take Home Task

Self-assessment Quiz

Part One

Stop! Think! Reflect!

How much we accept and like ourselves often impacts on how much we accept and like others. Stop and reflect! Think about your own qualities and feelings. Rate yourself against the following statements (0 = not often 5 = quite often 10 = all the time.)

I feel happy

1 2 3 4 5 6 7 8 9 10

I am generous

1 2 3 4 5 6 7 8 9 10

I am loyal

1 2 3 4 5 6 7 8 9 10

I am reliable

1 2 3 4 5 6 7 8 9 10

I am friendly and sociable

1 2 3 4 5 6 7 8 9 10

I am confident

1 2 3 4 5 6 7 8 9 10

I feel affectionate

1 2 3 4 5 6 7 8 9 10

I try hard

1 2 3 4 5 6 7 8 9 10

I work hard

1 2 3 4 5 6 7 8 9 10

Take Home Task

Self-assessment Quiz

Part One

I am honest

1 2 3 4 5 6 7 8 9 10

I am co-operative

1 2 3 4 5 6 7 8 9 10

I am considerate

1 2 3 4 5 6 7 8 9 10

I feel adventurous

1 2 3 4 5 6 7 8 9 10

I am a good listener

1 2 3 4 5 6 7 8 9 10

I feel positive

1 2 3 4 5 6 7 8 9 10

I am kind

1 2 3 4 5 6 7 8 9 10

I am sensitive

1 2 3 4 5 6 7 8 9 10

I am popular

1 2 3 4 5 6 7 8 9 10

I feel liked

1 2 3 4 5 6 7 8 9 10

I keep my cool

1 2 3 4 5 6 7 8 9 10

Take Home Task

Self-assessment Quiz

Part Two

Box 1

List the five qualities and feelings you rated highest:

1. ______
2. ______
3. ______
4. ______
5. ______

Box 2

List the five qualities and feelings you rated lowest:

1. ______
2. ______
3. ______
4. ______
5. ______

Go up the ladder! Record your current ratings for the qualities and feelings identified in Box 2. Then say where you'd like to be on the scale for each of these in the future.

Feeling or quality	Current rating	Preferred future rating
1.		
2.		
3.		
4.		
5.		

Give yourself a gift! Think about how you can achieve these preferred future ratings by identifying the following:

Things you can do to help yourself.

Things others can do to help you.

Things that can be changed around you to help you.

How do you know when you've reached your preferred future rating, i.e. what will be different? How differently will you feel?

Record your ideas on the back of this sheet.

Session 4

Feeling Positive

Introduction

In this session the students are able to focus on feeling positive and the importance of maintaining a positive attitude in order to maintain levels of motivation and achieve success. The first activity encourages the students to further develop positive relationships with each other via the Fact Finders Bingo activity whilst the second activity reinforces the importance of keeping positive both about oneself and about the other people one encounters in a range of contexts. The focus here is upon looking, speaking and acting positive in order to succeed and achieve personal goals. The subsequent activity encourages the students to analyse their own comments in order to assess levels of negativity and attempt to turn negatives into positives. The final activity encourages the students to make a commitment to remain positive and to practise positive thinking strategies on a daily basis. At the start of the session the facilitator can write up the following definition on the whiteboard or flip-chart:

Feeling positive is when you feel good about yourself and generally enjoy life and the experiences you encounter along the way.

Icebreaker

This icebreaker is entitled Positive Partners. The students should be arranged in pairs and each partner then articulates five positive feelings that they have about themselves at this current moment. Each partner articulates their own feelings and these are then fed back to the group as a whole via the circle. In order to save any embarrassment it would be helpful for partners to feedback for each other, i.e. they are not being asked to expose their own feelings to the rest of the group.

Questions for Circle Time

At this part of the session the students can focus upon the following questions:

- What does feeling positive actually mean?
- How have we experienced this feeling?
- When have we not felt positive?
- When people don't feel positive what do we think happens to their behaviour?
- How can we show others that we accept and like them?
- Why is it important to accept ourselves and remain motivated and positive?

Activity 1 – Fact Finding Bingo

This activity requires the students to individually complete the Fact Finding Bingo card. This can be photocopied prior to the start of the session onto A4 card as opposed to paper. The students will be required to move around the room and a sheet of paper might well get damaged. The students are asked to complete the chart by talking to everyone else in the group and finding at least one person who meets the criteria for a particular box. That person then has to sign the box and the students are required to continue this process until everyone in the group has filled in as many boxes as possible.

This activity is meant to be fun but also encourages the students to utilise social skills in completing each of the boxes, i.e. they have to ask questions, and listen to one another and co-operate effectively in order to complete the activity.

Activity 2 – Positive comments

This activity encourages the students to be positive about themselves and about the people they may meet. This is important because a positive attitude will help a student to succeed and achieve his or her goals. It will also ensure that others feel positive about them as well. The students are asked to make a positive comment about the person on their left, the person on their right and the person who is sitting opposite them. They are then required to ask each person to make their response in the response box. The students are asked to think about and analyse how each of the individuals responded to receiving a compliment from them. For example, were they happy, smiling, fidgeting, looking away or embarrassed? They are also asked to define a good response to receiving a positive comment and to suggest what would not be a good response and why this would be the case. Finally, they are asked to act out both kinds of responses, a poor response might include fidgeting, looking away or denying the compliment, and so on.

Activity 3 – No put downs, please!

This activity highlights the fact that we can make ourselves feel negative when we talk ourselves down. This is an extremely easy thing to do and a habit which we may have got into without quite realising it. The students are encouraged to stop and think every time they hear themselves making use of a put down and to try and turn this into a positive comment. The activity requires them to reverse a range of put downs into positive comments or statements. For example, "I was so lucky to pass the maths test because I worked extremely hard and put a lot of work in."

Take home task – Keep yourself positive, make a commitment now!

This task requires the students to complete the Feeling Positive chart by identifying five things they can say to themselves in order to keep positive, five things they can do in order to look positive and five things they can do in order to be positive. The focus here is on emphasising how what we say, how we look and how we act can have an impact upon our feelings and produce both positive and negative outcomes for ourselves.

Plenary

The brainstorming approach can be used in order to address the following questions:

- What have we learnt about this particular feeling?
- What have we learnt about how we experience this feeling?
- Have we learnt about how others experience this feeling?
- Are there any new concepts or language that we have learnt?
- Are there any new skills that we have been able to identify?
- How will this session impact upon us now and in the future?

Fact Finding Bingo

Complete Fact Finding Bingo by talking to everyone in the group. Find at least one person who meets the criteria for a box. That person then has to sign the box. Carry on until everyone in the group has filled in as many boxes as possible.

Is good at football	Has met someone famous	Can speak another language
Likes using a Playstation	Enjoys listening to music	Was born in March
Can play a musical instrument	Likes warm weather	Has a pet
Enjoys watching movies	Is good at maths	Has at least one brother
Is a good swimmer	Is a Sagittarian	Has blonde hair
Likes the same food as you	Has a tattoo	Is good at art
Loves pizza	Is good at writing	Has a computer

Positive Comments

Look positive

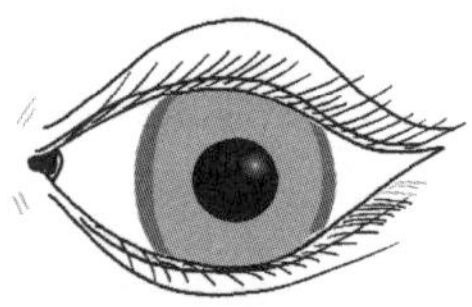

Speak positive

Act positive.

Be positive about yourself and about the people you meet. Your attitude will help you to succeed and achieve your goals. You will also ensure that others feel positive about themselves!

Make a positive comment about:

a. The person on your left
b. The person on your right
c. The person opposite you.

Then ask each person to write their response in the response box.

	Positive Comment	Response
a.		
b.		
c.		

Questions to discuss and think about

- How did each person respond to receiving a compliment? For example, smiling, happy, fidgeting, looking away, embarrassed.
- What is a good response to receiving a positive compliment?
- What would not be a good response and why?
- Can you 'act out' both kinds of responses, for example a poor response might include fidgeting, looking away or denying the compliments and so on.

No Put Downs, Please!

We can make ourselves feel negative when we talk ourselves down. It's an easy thing to do. What we need to do is stop and think every time we hear ourselves use a put down then try to turn it into a positive comment. Have a go at turning the following put downs into positive comments.

I was so lucky to pass the maths test.

I ....

I only got the prize because the teacher felt sorry for me.

I ....

I'm useless at all sports because I'm so fat.

I ....

People never ask me out.

People ....

I hate my face. It's so fat and spotty.

I ....

My parents or carers will never think I'm good at anything.

I ....

Everyone in my form is better looking than me.

I ....

I can't really expect to pass my exam because I'm not clever.

I ....

I always come last.

I ....

Remember! Keep positive. Just stop and think and monitor your put downs!

Take Home Task

Keep Yourself Positive!

Make a commitment – now complete your personal pledge chart!

Say

Five things I can say to myself to keep positive:

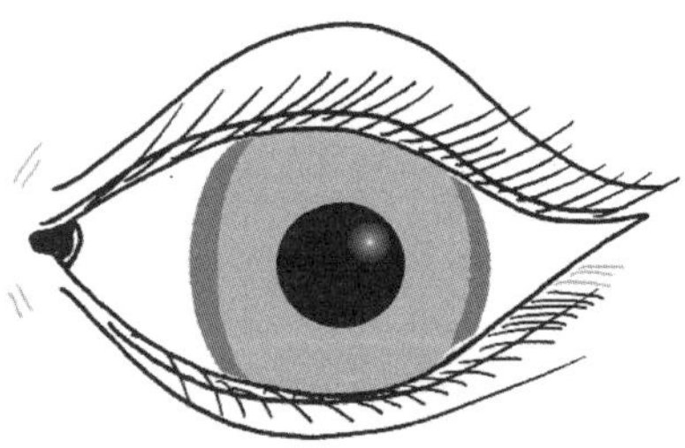

Look

Five things I can do to look positive:

Act

Five things I can do to be positive:

Once you've made your list, have a go! Tick off each statement as you go through the week and then feedback to the group at the start of the next session.

Session 5

Feeling Threatened

Introduction

This session focuses on feeling threatened and emphasises the fact that this is an experience common to most people. The students are asked to identify situations and events which may have caused them to feel threatened in the past alongside analysing their most positive responses to such threatening situations. There is also an opportunity for the students to rank a series of threats in order of seriousness. This activity intends to engender discussion as to the person specific nature of some threats to both our self-esteem and safety. There is also a particular focus upon threats to our self-esteem and how these can engender extremely negative reactions in terms of our behaviour. Finally, the students are required to identify personal threats alongside the ways in which they might effectively deal with these in the future.

The facilitator can write up the initial definition for feeling threatened on the whiteboard or flip-chart in order to then elicit the students personal definitions as to what they consider the feeling of threat to be and how they experience this particular feeling. The definition is as follows:

Feeling threatened is when you feel scared and frightened and that things or people are against you or out to get you.

Icebreaker

This icebreaker is entitled 'The Name Game'. The students can stand in a circle whilst the facilitator throws a ball to individuals who are required to give their name and then throw the ball back to the facilitator. The students can initially do this in a seated position in the circle and then move to a standing position if appropriate. The game can be further advanced by the students saying each other's names and passing it to different people in the circle alongside encouraging movement around the ball where the students can mirror each other's movements.

Questions for Circle Time

During this part of the session the students can focus upon the following questions:

- What do we mean by feeling threatened?
- What has made you feel threatened and say why.
- How do you know when someone else feels threatened?
- Can you name some positive responses to a threat?
- Can you name some negative responses to a threat?
- Does everyone feel threatened at some point and do they experience this in the same way?

Activity 1 – Feeling threatened

This activity introduces feeling threatened as an experience common to everyone. This is important in that all of the students need to recognise that it is not a sign of weakness to admit to such feelings and the facilitator needs to be persistent in dealing with any macho element or viewpoint which suggests that, for example, "I don't feel threatened by anyone." All of us can feel threatened by others by a variety of difficult situations and conflicts that we may experience on a daily basis. The students are asked to identify five things that have caused them to feel threatened and to record these on the brainstorming sheet provided. They are then required to give each set a rating from 1-3 for how serious the threat actually was at the time, 1 being very serious, 2 being quite serious and 3 being not very serious. The students are then required to identify their most positive responses to a threat and to analyse why their behaviour was more positive.

Activity 2 – Threat cards

The students are provided with a series of twelve cards each of which contains a threatening situation. It will be helpful for the facilitator to have photocopied these onto A4 card and to have cut these out prior to the session. However, if time is unavailable to do this then the students can simply work from photocopied sheets. The students are required to work in small groups and to rank the differnt situations in order, placing the biggest threat first and the smallest threat last. Each group is then required to feedback to the whole group and explain their reasons for ranking the situations in this particular way.

Activity 3 – Damon's diary

In this activity the students are required to read Damon's diary for last Monday. You should then ask them to work in groups in order to discuss a series of questions provided on the sheet and to attempt to reach agreement in their responses to each of these questions. This activity encourages the students to consider how others can cause us to feel threatened and how some threats are particularly painful in terms of attacking our self-esteem and confidence. The students are, required to work together in order to find a solution to a series of problems that they might well have experienced themselves.

Take Home Task – Personal threats

This activity requires the students to reflect upon and articulate the four main threats to their self-esteem, confidence and safety. Once this has been done they are then asked to consider how they could deal more effectively with these threats and what they could do to achieve a more positive outcome for themselves. This process also involves identifying people who may be able to help them. The idea here is to reinforce the fact that stopping, thinking and planning can often help to prevent further problems arising in the future.

Plenary

The brainstorming approach can be used in order to address the following questions:

- What have we learnt about this particular feeling?
- What have we learnt about how we experience this feeling?
- Have we learnt about how others experience this feeling?
- Are there any new concepts that we have learnt?
- Are there any new skills that we have been able to identify?
- How will this session impact upon us now and in the future?

Feeling Threatened

Feeling threatened is an experience common to everyone. We can feel threatened by others and by a variety of difficult situations and conflicts that we experience on a daily basis. Identify five things that have caused you to feel threatened and record your ideas on this brainstorming sheet.

Now give each threat a rating from 1 to 3 for how serious the threat actually was.

1 = very serious 2 = quite serious 3 = not very serious.

What was your most positive response to a threat? Why?

Record your ideas overleaf!

Threat Cards

Each of the twelve cards contains a threatening situation. Work in a small group and order these putting the biggest threat first and the smallest threat last then feedback to the whole group and explain your reasons for ranking them in this way.

The President of the United States has declared war on Great Britain.	Jason has started a new school but three boys in his form have made racist comments to him and he feels really scared.
Samantha's best friend has said that she wants to go out with the boy that Samantha really likes.	Carol's Mum has got a new boyfriend but Carol feels that he's creepy and doesn't feel comfortable on her own with him.
The maths GCSE exam is next week and Carl's Dad says he won't get any pocket money for a year if he fails.	Mr and Mrs Khaman have moved into a new house in a mainly white area of town. Yesterday somebody pushed Mrs Khaman over in the street as she went to the Post Office.

Threat Cards

Terrorists have been planting bombs on public transport facilities in London and other major cities in the UK.	Seymeem's Dad wants her to have an arranged marriage and says that he will turn her out of the house if she doesn't do as he says.
Paul's brother is taking drugs and always needs money to feed his habit. He's asked for Paul's savings four times now.	Mr Armitage's boss has said that he'll sack him if he's late for work again.
Jacqueline's boyfriend has said that he'll ditch her if she doesn't have sex with him. She's 14 and thinks she's too young.	Lara's Head of Year has said that she will be permanently excluded if she continues to behave so badly.

Damon's Diary

Read Damon's diary for last Monday then work in a group and discuss the questions. Can you reach agreements about your answers?

Monday

Dear Diary,

I've had a really bad day today. I got up late again and Mum said that if I did that again then she'd stop giving me a lift to school and I'd have to get the bus. Then she said, "Tough - you'll have to get the bus anyway!" and left - just like that! I don't know what got into her. Anyway, on the bus two Year 11 kids stopped and said that they'd beat me up if I didn't hand over my lunch money. I felt so stupid. But what could I do - they were twice my size and I don't have any mates who can help. At least, they weren't on the bus. So, I didn't have any lunch because I couldn't pay for it and I ended up stealing a packet of crisps from the tuck shop but Mrs Butler caught me and gave me a detention plus she's sending a note home to Mum saying that I'm a thief!

That'll just about finish off my relationship with her - she definitely won't be speaking to me for at least a month - the silent and violent treatment of course. Anyway, I'll stop going on now as there's nothing I can do, is there?

Yours, Damon

Why was Damon's mum so angry and fed up with him?

What did Damon mean when he said, "I felt so stupid"? What kind of threat did the two Year 11 boys really pose?

What do you think that Damon could have done instead of stealing the crisps?

How do you think he feels about the letter going home to his Mum?

Is there anything Damon could do in order to achieve a better outcome?

Take Home Task

Personal Threats

Start with yourself! What do you consider to be the four main threats to your self-esteem, confidence and safety? Record your ideas below.

1. ....
....
2. ....
....
3. ....
....
4. ....
....

Stop, think and plan. How can you effectively deal with these threats? What can you do in order to achieve a more positive outcome for yourself? Who can help you? Record your ideas below:

1. ....
....
2 ....
....
3. ....
....
4. ....
....

Work out what to do first and who may best be able to help you. Go for it!

Session 6

Feeling Angry

Introduction

This session focuses upon how the students experience the feeling of anger and introduces ways in which they may be able to cope with this often uncomfortable feeling more effectively. The students are asked to consider how they feel both physically and emotionally when they experience difficult situations and to compare their responses with members of their peer group alongside identifying a range of anger spoilers and self-management strategies and techniques. They are introduced to a stepped approach to managing anger and are encouraged to act out a range of difficult situations in which they may be able to utilise such an approach. Anger is also presented as a secondary feeling which they may experience subsequent to feeling such emotions as fear, shame or jealousy. This is important in that it aims to show the students how a range of feelings will produce angry responses alongside the importance of being able to analyse these feelings and to inhibit these responses when appropriate. The students are asked to keep a personal anger diary for one week in order to identify their own triggers and to consequently be able to more effectively deal with these and recognise these as their curve on a regular basis.

The facilitator can write up the initial definition for feeling threatened on the whiteboard or flip-chart in order to then elicit the students' personal definitions as to what they consider the feeling of threat to be and how they experience this particular feeling. The definition is as follows:

Feeling angry is when you get upset and stressed by another person or situation and this can lead you to become physically or verbally aggressive.

Icebreaker

This activity is entitled 'The Frozen Lake'. The students are asked to imagine that they are on a frozen lake and to then act out how they would move and to identify what they would say and feel in this situation.

The facilitator can do this activity simultaneously with the students and further develop it along the lines of:

- Imagine you are in a pit full of snakes.
- Imagine you are in a vat full of jelly.
- Imagine you are in a dark box, and so on.

This activity encourages the students to express themselves both verbally and non-verbally and to identify the range of feelings that they may experience in each situation.

Questions at Circle Time

During this part of the session the students can focus upon the following questions:

- What is anger?
- Why do we feel angry?
- Is anger always negative or can it be positive?
- When would it be right to feel angry?

- What kind of responses do people have when they feel angry?
- How can we manage our own anger so that it doesn't generate negative outcomes?
- How do we know when others are angry with us?
- Can we help each other to control and manage our anger more effectively?

Activity 1 – Feeling angry

This activity requires the students to assess their own angry feelings and to identify how they act when they experience such feelings. They are required to tick against a range of statements that may or may not apply to them.

The students are then required to compare their responses with either the person sitting next to them or a partner and to analyse whether these are the same or different and why this may or may not be the case.

Activity 2 – How Can I Cope with my Angry Feelings?

This activity requires the students to identify their own personal strategies for coping with angry feelings and introduces a range of anger spoilers.

The students are asked to tick against the strategies that they feel might be useful or work for them. It may also be helpful for the facilitator to describe the traffic light method in more detail. This can be found in *Dealing With Feelings* and *Dealing With Some More Feelings* (Lucky Duck Publishing).

Activity 3 – Don't Light the Fuse

This activity introduces the students to a stepped approach to solving problems.

It will be important for the students to discuss this and to consider how this may be useful for them. They are then required to act out a range of situations and to attempt to make use of this stepped approach in order to make a positive response to each of the situations presented.

The students are asked to act out their scenes to the whole group and then to think of a personal anger trigger and try to find the solution to this.

Activity 4 – A Aecondary Feeling?

This activity introduces the idea that prior to becoming angry people often experience other feelings such as fear, shame or jealousy. The students are required to identify the primary feelings for each of the problems listed on the sheet and to record them in the relevant boxes. For example, you couldn't understand the work – this may initially result in you feeling ashamed, stressed, unhappy and embarrassed and this may then lead on to the secondary feeling of anger which may be expressed in a negative way.

Take Home Task – Personal anger triggers

This activity asks the students to keep a diary for one week and to record each situation or time when they became angry. The idea here is to encourage the students to develop their own awareness of their personal triggers to anger and to attempt to identify ways in which they may avoid such situations or deal with them more effectively.

Plenary

The brainstorming approach can be used in order to address the following questions:

- What have we learnt about this particular feeling?
- What have we learnt about how we experience this feeling?
- Have we learnt about how others experience this feeling?
- Are there any new concepts that we have learnt?
- Are there any new skills that we have been able to identify?
- How will this session impact upon us now and in the future?

Feeling Angry

Assess yourself! How do you feel when you get angry and how do you act? Tick against the statements that apply to you.

Feelings	Actions
I feel hot and shaky	I scream
My body feels tight and rigid	I shout
I feel panicked	I lash out
My mouth is dry	I run away
My fists are clenched	I punch back
My hands become sweaty	I throw things
My breathing is faster	I swear
My heart beats quickly	I cry

Compare your responses with the person sitting next to you. Are they the same or different? Discuss why you think this might be.

How Can I Cope with My Angry Feelings?

Danny has completed half of this brainstorm activity. What else would you suggest he could try? What are your strategies? Complete the chart below.

Tick against the strategies that you feel might work for you. Go on! Try them out!

Don't Light the Fuse!

Do's:

Stop and wait until you've calmed down a bit.

Listen to the other person (even if you disagree).

Say how you feel clearly.

Provide a solution – say how it could be better or different.

Act it out

Choose one of the anger triggers below. Work in pairs or small groups and act out the situation. Work out a positive response using the 'do's' so that you dampen that fuse! Show your scene to the rest of the group.

The teacher has accused you of talking and it wasn't you.

You've been left out of the team because the captain doesn't like you.

An older boy has made a racist comment to your best friend.

Your best friend has gone off with someone else and left you out.

Your parents or carers refuse to let you go to the party and all your friends are going.

The teacher shouted at you for not giving in your homework.

Kids in your class have started dissing your mum.

Your big sister won't let you play your music.

Think of a 'personal anger trigger' and try to find a solution.

Record your ideas on the reverse of the sheet.

A Secondary Feeling?

Before they get angry, people often experience other feelings such as fear, shame or jealousy. Try to identify the secondary feelings for each of the problems below and record them in the relevant boxes.

Take Home Task

Personal Anger Triggers

Keep your diary for one week and then work out your major triggers.

Trigger	Action	Outcome
Sunday		
Monday		
Tuesday		
Wednesday		
Thursday		
Friday		
Saturday		

Which strategies can you use to avoid lighting the fuse? Record your ideas on the reverse of this sheet.

Session 7

Feeling Stressed

Introduction

This session focuses upon identifying the main causes of stress and encourages the students to consider how they manage their own stressors. There is also a focus upon the person specific nature of stress and the ways in which individuals can experience stress differently from each other. The students are encouraged to consider a range of stress management strategies and to identify those which appear to work best for them.

The facilitator can write up the initial definition for stress on the whiteboard or flip-chart in order to then elicit the students' personal definitions as to what they consider stress to be and how they experience stress. The definition is as follows:

Feeling stressed is when you feel that you have too much pressure put upon you and you can't cope with things any more.

Icebreaker

This icebreaker is entitled 'Four Feelings'. This activity is set up for a Circle Time session. The facilitator identifies four feelings. For example, lonely, excited, furious, friendly. Each student is then labelled with a feeling state in order around the circle. The facilitator then calls out one feeling and all those who have been labelled with that feeling must change places. When four feelings are called everyone changes places.

Questions for Circle Time

During this part of the session the students can focus upon the following questions:

- What do we mean by stress?
- What has made you feel stressed and why.
- How do you know when others feel stressed?
- Can you name some positive responses to stress?
- Can you name some negative responses to stress?
- Does everyone experience stress and do they experience it in the same way?

Activity 1 – Feeling stressed brainstorm

The students are required to articulate their own definitions for stress and to identify who gets stressed and what causes this stress. They can work in a small group or a pair during this brainstorming activity. Subsequent to this the students are asked to make lists of their own personal stressors on the reverse of the worksheet. They are then encouraged to discuss these with a partner and to identify any similarities or differences between their stresses. This is intended to highlight to the students that stress really can be person specific.

Activity 2 – Stress cards

It will be useful for the facilitator to have photocopied these onto card so that the students can then cut out the cards more easily in order to complete the activity. The students should be encouraged to work in groups of four or five and to discuss each of the stresses so as to then agree a rank order for each situation, for example, placing the most stressful situation at the top and the least stressful situation at the bottom. It will be interesting to see how the students reach any agreement and if they consider any of these stresses to have equal significance. Once again, the intention here is to point out the person specific nature of stress whilst also highlighting that some stresses will cause nearly everybody significant difficulties, for example, a bereavement, being bullied or being poor.

Activity 3 Stress busters!

This activity encourages the students to consider a range of stress busters and to identify those that they currently use and those that they may consider using in the future.

It may also be helpful to encourage the students to identify personal stress busters which they may have found helpful and may also be of use to other people in the class.

Take Home Task My stress buster plan

This activity requires the students to reflect upon the first activity and to identify the three main stresses they would like to deal with at this current moment. They can then identify which of the strategies might help best in each case and attempt to visualise how they will know if or when these strategies have worked. This visualising of what life will be like without the problem is based on solution focused thinking and encourages the students to adopt a positive and pro-active approach towards their stressors.

Plenary

The brainstorming approach can be used in order to address the following questions:

- What have we learnt about this particular feeling?
- What have we learnt about how we experience this feeling?
- Have we learnt about how others experience this feeling?
- Are there any new concepts that we have learnt?
- Are there any new skills that we have been able to identify?
- How will this session impact upon us now and in the future?

Feeling Stressed

What is stress? What causes stress? Who gets stressed? Consider these questions.

Work in small groups or pairs and record your ideas on this brainstorm sheet.

Make a list of your 'personal stressors' on the reverse of this sheet.
Then discuss them with a partner. Are there similarities and differences?
Is stress person specific?

Stress Cards

Driving	Queuing up	Being bullied at school
Having an argument with a friend	Going to see the Head Teacher	Meeting new people
Moving house	Pressure to have sex	Joining a club
Losing a job	Pressure to do drugs	Thinking about school
Being poor	Tidying the house	Teachers picking on you
Going on holiday	Learning a job	Not having the 'right' clothes
Exams	Christmas	Being ill
Death in the family	Leaving school	Thinking about work
Divorce	Being bullied at work	Getting behind with coursework.
Pet dying	Home being burgled	Babysitting

Cut out the stress cards and then work in a group to rank these situations – which is the most stressful? Can you agree in your group or does stress really seem to be different for each individual?

Stress Busters!

Look at the list of stress busters and tick against those that you currently use and then tick against those that you would consider using in the future.

Stress buster	Using now	Could use in future
Talking it through with a friend		
Keeping fit		
Being assertive		
Being positive and looking for a solution		
Keeping a balance between work and leisure		
Relaxation and meditation strategies		
Treating yourself		
Learning a new skill		
Listening to music		
Taking a nap		
Deep breathing		
Yoga		
Taking 'time out'		

Share your plan with a partner or friend. Can you also support each other in the process?

Remember – keep a positive attitude! If it doesn't work and you know it went wrong, then develop a new plan and try again!

Go for it!

Take Home Task

My Stress Buster Plan

Look back to the first 'Feeling Stressed' activity and identify the three main stressors that you'd like to deal with now. Consider which strategies might help best in each case and then visualise how you will know if the strategies have worked. Complete the table below.

Main Stressor	Strategies I could use	What will change? How will I know if it's worked?
1.		
2.		
3.		

Share your plan with a partner or friend. Can you also support each other in the process?

Remember – keep a positive attitude!

If it doesn't work and you know what went wrong, then develop a new plan and try again! Go for it!

Session 8

Feeling Assertive

Introduction

This session focuses on feeling assertive and clarifies the distinction between assertive, aggressive and passive behaviours and responses. The students are encouraged to utilise a calm, reflective and stepped approach to solving difficult problems. There is opportunity for the students to work in small groups and act out assertive, aggressive and passive responses to a range of problem situations that they may well experience on a daily basis. The students are also introduced to the five rules for negotiation and encouraged to utilise a negotiation framework in order to solve a problem. Finally, the students are encouraged to reflect carefully upon their own skills and to identify specific targets in order to increase their level of assertiveness and assertive responses in the school and home context. The facilitator can make use of the whiteboard or flip-chart in order to elicit the students' definitions and to provide an initial definition as follows :

Feeling assertive is when you feel strong and calm and you can ask for what you want without hurting or abusing others.

Icebreaker

This icebreaker is entitled 'Who Is It?' The facilitator nominates one person to leave the room. Whilst this student is out of the room the facilitator nominates another student to be 'it'. The first returns to the room and is encouraged to ask questions of his or her classmates in order to find out who is 'it'. The students are only allowed to answer 'yes', 'no', or 'don't know' and this continues until the student has been able to guess the identity correctly. It may be helpful to make a limit of three guesses!

Questions for Circle Time

During this part of the session the students can focus upon the following questions:

- What is meant by feeling assertive?
- What is meant by feeling aggressive?
- What is meant by feeling passive?
- When were you last assertive?
- When were you last passive?
- When were you last aggressive?

Say how you feel now in an assertive way, a passive way and an aggressive way.

What ideas do you have for coping with someone else who is aggressive towards you?

Activity 1 - Feeling assertive

This activity highlights to the students that when they are feeling assertive they are usually able to say what they mean so that people will listen to them. This will usually entail them being and feeling calm and in control. The students are asked to work with a partner in order to complete the definitions chart on these three feeling states. It is important that they identify how someone would look and sound, feel and behave when experiencing such a feeling.

The students are encouraged to share their own experiences with a partner and to discuss particularly the resulting behaviours. The focus here is on self-reflection and the students are asked to consider why they responded in a particular way to a particular situation and to further reflect on whether or not they could have responded differently to achieve a better outcome.

Activity 2 Role-play cards

The facilitator should photocopy the handouts onto card prior to the beginning of the session and ideally it would be helpful if these could have been cut out and laminated for convenience and ease of use both for now and in the future. The students are placed into small groups and required to act out responses to each of the problem situations. The distinction between assertive, aggressive and passive responses is reinforced. It is important to note that this is not a particularly easy activity and that the students really will have to think about what they are going to say as well as how they look, how they stand and how they sound to the other person. Noting and observing each other's body language is vital as it is interesting to consider how much our body language can or cannot intimidate others.

Activity 3 Assertively negotiate!

The importance of what we say and how we say it is reinforced in this activity. The students are introduced to five rules for negotiation and it is emphasised how important being able to negotiate with others is in order to sort out problems and deal with conflicts effectively.

This stepped approach, utilises a solution focused strategy and is consistent with the traffic light method introduced to both problem-solve and cope more effectively with angry feelings. The students are required to work in pairs in order to identify a current or recent conflict and to then make use of the negotiation framework in order to practise their skills. The negotiation framework simply makes use of the five rules for negotiation and requires the students to articulate their needs, feelings and thoughts alongside identifying appropriate solutions.

Take Home Task Self-reflection

The activity encourages the students to reflect upon their own skills and to assess the current level of their assertive behaviours and responses. The students are asked to identify where their lowest ratings were against each statement and to then consider how they might improve on these particular areas. The scaling process used is made clear on the activity sheet and the students are encouraged to make use of this visual tool in order to visualise and articulate preferred ratings and future targets.

Plenary

The brainstorming approach can be used in order to address the following questions:

- What have we learnt about this particular feeling?
- What have we learnt about how we experience this feeling?
- Have we learnt about how others experience this feeling?
- Are there any new concepts that we have learnt?
- Are there any new skills that we have been able to identify?
- How will this session impact upon us now and in the future?

Feeling Assertive

If you are assertive you can say what you mean so that people will listen to you. You won't need to be aggressive or passive. You will be calm and in control. Stop and think! Work with a partner and try to complete the definitions chart.

Definitions	How do you look and sound?	How do you feel?	What tends to happen?
Being assertive means			
Being aggressive means			
Being passive means			

Think and discuss with your partner. When have you felt and been assertive, aggressive or passive? Describe the situations and try to work out why you responded in this way? How could you have responded differently?

Role-play Cards

Work in small groups and act out an assertive, an aggressive and a passive response to these problem situations.

The maths teacher has wrongly accused you of copying your friend's answers.	People are bullying your friend because she's clever and works hard.
Your Mum won't let you go to the party because she's worried that people will be taking drugs.	You're been asked to tidy up the art room but the rest of the group are leaving all the work to you.
Your boyfriend or girlfriend wants to have sex with you but you're not ready.	Someone has taken your mobile phone and is making a call without your permission.
You lost your homework but the teacher doesn't believe you.	People are criticising your new clothes.
Alcohol makes you feel sick but all your friends will slag you off if you don't drink.	Someone has taken your magazine and ripped out four pages.
It's your turn on the computer and you need to order a book on the Internet but your brother won't let you have a go.	You got a detention for mucking about in class but you really weren't involved.

Assertively Negotiate!

When we feel and act assertively we can negotiate with others in order to sort out problems and deal with conflicts. We can follow the five rules for negotiation:

- Say what you want and why.
- Say what you think the other person wants and why.
- Identify some solutions.
- Choose one solution.
- Check it out – does it suit everyone?

In pairs identify a current or recent conflict and use the negotiation framework to practise your skills.

Remember to give your reasons and keep assertive.

Negotiation Framework

Step1: I want ______________________________

Because ______________________________

____

Step 2: I think you want ______________________________

Because ______________________________

____

Step 3: These are my suggested solutions: ______________________________

____

Step 4: Let's agree to try: ______________________________

____

Step 5: Do we agree and does it suit us both? ______________________________

____

Go for it!

Take Home Task

Self-reflection Activity

How assertive are you? Rate yourself against the following statements:

(1 = never, 5 = sometimes, 10 = always)

I can stop myself getting angry and use anger blockers.

I don't swear or call people names if I'm in an argument.

1 2 3 4 5 6 7 8 9 10

I can speak calmly if I feel upset.

1 2 3 4 5 6 7 8 9 10

I can use assertive body language (shoulders back, head high).

1 2 3 4 5 6 7 8 9 10

I can keep a low, even voice and speak clearly when I need to.

1 2 3 4 5 6 7 8 9 10

I can say how I feel.

1 2 3 4 5 6 7 8 9 10

I can say what I want.

1 2 3 4 5 6 7 8 9 10

I don't use threatening body language or words.

1 2 3 4 5 6 7 8 9 10

I can maintain eye contact when I'm saying something.

1 2 3 4 5 6 7 8 9 10

I can say why I feel like I do.

1 2 3 4 5 6 7 8 9 10

I can listen to someone else's point of view.

1 2 3 4 5 6 7 8 9 10

I can say calmly what I'd like to happen and why.

1 2 3 4 5 6 7 8 9 10

Where are your lowest ratings? How can you improve these? Identify and discuss your targets with a friend or significant adult. Ask if they would give you the same ratings for each statement and consider why they may or may not agree.

Session 9

Feeling Listened To

Introduction

This session focuses on promoting listening behaviours and highlights the importance of maintaining good eye contact, appropriate body language, allowing personal space requirements, turn-taking skills, non-verbal behaviours and their importance in communication alongside the importance of developing empathy. The students are asked to participate in a range of role-play activities in which they demonstrate both appropriate and inappropriate listening behaviours. They are also then required to consider the kinds of feelings they experience when they are evidently not being listened to and the feelings they may or may not engender in others when they appear not to be listening to others. The students are encouraged to consider how they adjust their facial expression, head movements, posture, spatial distance, eye contact and use of voice to indicate that they have good communication skills. They are finally required to self-reflect upon their own skills and to consider ways in which they may be able to become better listeners.

The facilitator can write up the initial definition for feeling threatened on the whiteboard or flip-chart in order to then elicit the students' personal definitions as to what they consider the feeling of threat to be and how they experience this particular feeling. The definition is as follows:

Feeling listened to is when you know that someone is really hearing what you have to say and not ignoring your feelings or point of view.

Icebreaker

This icebreaker is entitled 'Who Are You?' Collect pictures of famous people such as pop stars, television personalities, film stars and so on. These pictures will be sticky taped onto the students' backs. Obviously, the students will not have seen these pictures. The students can then walk around the room while others question them about these 'names' until each student is able to guess the character on their back! It may be necessary to repeat the initial rules or ground rules at this point. Once the students have guessed the character the facilitator can then ask them to arrange themselves for a circle session and ask the following questions:

- What do you feel about your character and why?

Questions for Circle Time

During this part of the session the students can focus upon the following questions:

- How do you know when someone is listening to you?
- How do you show others that you are listening to them?
- What makes a good listener?
- What makes a bad listener?
- When did you listen well?
- When did you last feel not listened to?

Activity 1 – Feeling Listened To

The students are asked to brainstorm a range of questions.

It may be helpful prior to the start of this activity for the facilitator to discuss the key prompt words.

It will be important to formulate, or encourage the students to formulate, some sort of definition for each of these key words.

It will be particularly important to highlight the fact that non-verbal behaviours include gestures, facial expression, head movements, posture, fiddling movements, spatial distance, eye contact and voice.

Activity 2 – Secret Action Cards

The facilitator can photocopy these cards onto card before the start of the session in order to save time. The students should be placed into pairs and asked to engage in a conversation about a topic that particularly interests them, for example football, soap operas, clothes. The facilitator then gives one partner a card and asks them to silently read the directions and follow these through. After a few minutes, it will be interesting to elicit the students' views particularly those who did not receive the cards. How did they feel when their partner started to stare at them? How did they feel when their partner lent forward towards them? The idea here is to focus in on how our non-verbal behaviours can impact upon our listening skills and the way others perceive us to be listening or otherwise to their conversation.

Activity 3 – Listening Behaviours Checklist

This leads on directly from the previous activity, highlighting the importance of non-verbal behaviours. The students can be divided into groups of four with two individuals being directed to hold a conversation on a topic of their choice as in the previous activity. Whilst they are engaged in conversation the two remaining members of the group can make use of their listening behaviour checklist in order to assess each student's non-verbal behaviours. This should result in each student being able to identify the communication styles of the others and also in identifying three ways in which he or she may improve his or her skills in this area. Adequate time should be allowed so that the students can observe each other and participate in the conversation and be observed themselves.

Take Home Task – Do you listen? Blocking Behaviours.

This activity requires the students to consider the ways in which they may or may not block communication with their friends or family members. Each student is required to reflect upon his or her listening behaviours over the coming week to attempt to complete the chart.

Plenary

The brainstorming approach can be used in order to address the following questions:

- What have we learnt about this particular feeling?
- What have we learnt about how we experience this feeling?
- Have we learnt about how others experience this feeling?
- Are there any new concepts that we have learnt?
- Are there any new skills that we have been able to identify?
- How will this session impact upon us now and in the future?

Feeling Listened To

Brainstorm! Record your ideas to the questions on the Brainstorming chart.

How do you know when someone is listening to you?

How do you know when someone isn't listening to you?

How do you know when people don't listen to you?

What do you do when people don't listen to you?

How do you feel when people listen to you?

How do you behave when people listen to you?

How do you know when you're really listening to others, i.e. what are you doing, saying, thinking and feeling?

Key prompt words:

eye contact, personal space, non-verbal behaviours, body language, turn-taking, empathy

Secret Action Cards

Take part in the conversation but don't look at the person's eyes.	Listen to your partner but don't say a word.	Take part in the conversation but turn your body sideways on.
Take part in the conversation but keep yawning.	Take part in the conversation but stare at the other person all the time.	Take part in the conversation but lean right back in your chair.
Take part in the conversation but keep looking at your watch or the class clock.	Take part in the conversation but keep a very blank look on your face.	Take part in the conversation and smile and look interested throughout.
Take part in the conversation but continually scratch your ear.	Take part in the conversation but keep scratching your nose and blinking.	Take part in the conversation and continually nod your head to encourage your partner.
Take part in the conversation but keep pulling at your clothes.	Take part in the conversation and keep giving your partner good eye contact.	Take part in the conversation and lean forward when your partner speaks.
Take part in the conversation and try to mirror your partner's body language.	Take part in the conversation but continually fidget and look around the room.	Take part in the conversation but move your chair nearer to your partners.

Listening Behaviours Checklist

Name: ______________________________

Observed by: ______________________________

Highlight or circle the non-verbal behaviours you observed on the following list:

Gestures	A lot Some None	Smooth and controlled Jerky and uncontrolled Exaggerated	Very small
Facial expressions	Tense Relaxed Smiling	Frowning Blank Changes as other person speaks	
Head movements	Some	Lots	None
Posture	Leaning backwards Leaning forwards	Slouching Sitting up	Tense Relaxed
Fiddling movements	Some Lots None	Fidgeting Swinging legs Moving in seat	Scratching
Spatial distance	Close Too far away	Just right Made partner feel comfortable Made partner feel uncomfortable	
Eye contact	Some Lots None	Staring Looking around room	
Voice	Quiet Loud Medium	Slow Fast Mumbled	Clear Monotone Interesting

Does this person communicate well? Why?

How could he or she improve their skills? Make three suggestions:

1. ______________________________

2. ______________________________

3. ______________________________

Take Home Task

Do You Listen?

Blocking Behaviours

Do you listen to others or do you block communication? Reflect on your listening behaviours over the week and try and complete the chart below. (use a tick)

	Frequently	Often	Sometimes	Not often	Not at all
Put downns (making others feel down, bad or hurt)	☐	☐	☐	☐	☐
Self-talk (talking about yourself and not being interested in others)	☐	☐	☐	☐	☐
I know best (telling others what they should or shouldn't do)	☐	☐	☐	☐	☐
Cutting across (implementing)	☐	☐	☐	☐	☐
Interpreting (judging them and trying to put words in their mouths)	☐	☐	☐	☐	☐

Which blocking behaviour did you use the most?

____

Which didn't you use?

____

How can you become a better listener?

____

I could…

____

____

Session 10

Feeling in Control

Introduction

This session introduces the notion of locus of control. The students are encouraged to consider whether or not they take responsibility for their own behaviours, i.e. remain in control, or whether they blame others for their mistakes or misjudgements. This process also involves considering the part that luck may or may not play in their lives and the extent to which they may or may not feel controlled by others. This process involves the students in distinguishing between situations and responses which reflect internal or external control. There is also a focus upon the fact that everyone always has a choice to be in control or be controlled by others and the situation they find themselves in.

The facilitator can elicit the students' definitions and record these on the whiteboard or flip-chart after initially providing them with the following definition:

Feeling in control is when you know that you can cope and haven't lost it and that you are responsible for your own behaviours.

Icebreaker

This icebreaker is entitled 'Match the Colour'. The facilitator will have made up a range of coloured cards. He or she can then ask the students which emotion, state or feeling they would match to each of these colours. It may be helpful to record the students' ideas on a whiteboard or flip-chart under each colour heading and to nominate one student to act as a scribe for this activity. It may then be helpful to point out any differences and similarities in the students' responses.

Questions for Circle Time

At this part of the session the students can focus upon the following questions:

- How would you define feeling in control?
- When did you last take responsibility for your behaviours?
- Are you currently in control?
- When have you blamed someone else for your mistakes?
- Do you believe in luck and if so why?
- Who controls you or others?
- What does someone who's feeling in control look like, sound like and act like?

Activity 1 Feeling in control

This activity introduces the concepts of internal and external control and asks the students to consider five different things that they feel they have done well and to then record the reasons for these successes. Finally they are asked to decide if they feel that they had either internal or external control at these times in their lives. The majority of the students' successes will have occurred when they have had internal control. However, it will be interesting to discuss this in order to identify the students who feel that luck may have played a part in some of these successes.

Activity 2 – Sort it out. Who is in control?

It will be helpful for the facilitator to have photocopied the control cards onto A4 card prior to the start of the session so that the students can easily cut them out and make effective use of them during this activity. The students are required to work with a partner or in a small group in order to read through each of these cards and to sort them into two groups: those that show internal control and those that show external control. For example, "I messed around in the maths lesson because the teacher was boring," shows external control because the student is blaming the teacher for his or her behaviour, whereas, "I didn't do well on the test because I hadn't bothered to revise," shows internal locus of control as the student is saying that he or she was at fault for not having worked hard and therefore responsible entirely for the negative outcome.

Activity 3 – Who? Me? Thumbnail sketch

This worksheet focuses on the importance of the students having and taking choices in their lives. It may be helpful for the facilitator to read through the thumbnail sketch prior to the students completing the activity. The character in the thumbnail sketch identifies five situations in which he had a choice. The students are asked to advise on what the character should or should not have done in each of these situations. They are asked to identify the situation and then clarify the choices prior to identifying the best choice and the outcome of that choice. There is a focus on developing reflection skills and a stepped approach to solving problems.

Take Home Task – Self reflection activity

This activity asks the students to identify a critical moment for each day of the coming week. These will generally be situations where the students have a choice either to be in control or to be controlled by others or the situation. The students are asked to record their choices on the chart and then identify behaviours that they feel will lead to the best possible outcome. For example, a student might say that the critical moment on Sunday is when, "My Mum asks me to tidy my room because it's a mess and I don't want to." The internal control choice here would be "I will take responsibility and tidy up my room because I made the mess". The external control choice will be, "I don't want to do this because it wasn't my fault, my brother made most of this mess so why should I tidy it up?" The best possible outcome would be for the student to adopt the internal control choice. The idea here is to highlight how the internal control choices generally achieve a better outcome.

Plenary

The brainstorming approach can be used in order to address the following questions:

- What have we learnt about this particular feeling?
- What have we learnt about how we experience this feeling?
- Have we learnt about how others experience this feeling?
- Are there any new concepts that we have learnt?
- Are there any new skills that we have been able to identify?
- How will this session impact upon us now and in the future?

Internal control

Do you take responsibility for your behaviour? Are you in control?

External control

Do you blame others for your mistakes?

Do you think that luck plays a part in your life?

Are you controlled by others?

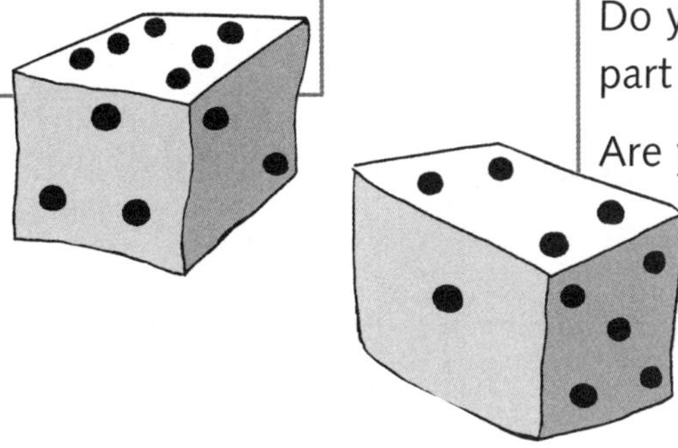

Think about five different things that you have done well. Record your reasons for your successes and then try to decide if you had either 'internal' or 'external' control at these times.

My success	Reasons for my success	External or internal control
1		
2		
3		
4		
5		

Sort it Out
Who is in Control?

Work with a partner in small groups. Read through the control cards and sort them into two groups: internal or external control

Control Cards

I messed around in the maths lesson because the teacher was boring.	I didn't do well on the test because I hadn't bothered to revise.
I got a good report for last term because my teachers were kinder and more relaxed.	I scored the goal because the goal-keeper dived the wrong way.
I was selected for the football team because the others were useless.	I didn't do well on the test because the questions were too hard.
Everyone was mucking about and I only got into trouble because the teacher saw me throw the bit of paper.	It was hard to get a place on the Quiz team but all the extra study and reading really paid off.

Control Cards

I don't usually beat my Dad at cards – he can't have been concentrating.	I bumped into her because I wasn't looking where I was going.
I did well because our group all helped each other and worked as a team.	People kept on saying I was fat and ugly so I had to hit them.
I always do well in tests if I use my lucky pen.	My Mum said my room was a mess but my little brother messed up most of it.
That teacher has never liked me and that's why I'm always in trouble in her lessons.	I lost the game because I wasn't paying attention.
Everyone was ignoring the fire alarm so I did too.	I didn't get into trouble because I managed to keep quiet and do my work.
Mr Bates thinks I'm stupid so I never work in his lessons.	I didn't shout back at Ella because I used my anger blockers well.

Who? Me?

Thumbnail Sketch

Danny can't accept responsibility for his actions. He always thinks his problems are down to someone else. Even when he's done something well he'll say it was just luck and not because he was any good or did well at something. He will never say, "I have a choice."

Look at the list of things he did on Monday.

9.00am	Late for school because he won't wait for a bus.
10.10am	Chucked out of maths because he was chatting and kept getting out of his seat.
12.30pm	Missed lunch because he left his money at home.
1.45pm	Got a detention because he didn't finish his English homework.
2.50pm	Bunked off the science lesson because he hadn't revised for the test.

Think carefully about these five situations. Danny clearly had a choice in each one. What would you advise him to do and why?

Record your ideas in four columns on the reverse of this sheet as follows. An example is provided for the first situation.

Danny's situation	Danny's choices	The 'best' choice	What will the outcome be?
Late for school.	Apologise. Leave at the same time and be late again. Get up earlier and catch an earlier bus.	Get up earlier.	Won't be late and stressed or in trouble.

Take Home Task

Self-reflection Activity

Identify one 'critical moment' for each day of the coming week. These will be situations where you have a choice to either be in control or controlled by others and the situation. Record your choices and identify the behaviours that will lead to the best possible outcome on the chart below.

	Critical moment	Internal control choice	External control choice	Best possible outcome
Saturday				
Friday				
Thursday				
Wednesday				
Tuesday				
Monday				
Sunday				

Stop and think! Do your internal control choices achieve a better outcome? If so, why do you think this happens?

Session 11

Feeling in Conflict

Introduction

This session focuses upon identifying the main sources of conflict that the students may be currently experiencing and introduces a problem-solving format for the students to utilise when engaged in a conflict with others. The three possible results of the conflict are also identified as being a win win situation, a win lose situation or a lose lose situation. The students are encouraged to identify the necessary skills for solving conflicts and ensuring win win situations and solutions for themselves. The final problem-solving format encourages the students to be reflective collectors of information and to communicate and co-operate in order to achieve win win situations.

The facilitator can elicit the students' personal definitions of conflict, and record these on a whiteboard or flip-chart subsequent to introducing the following definition:

Feeling in conflict is when you know that you disagree with someone and you don't want to give in and let them have their way as this will cause you to feel angry and stressed.

Icebreaker

This icebreaker is entitled 'Sign it!' The facilitator allocates the students a partner. The task is then for each student to try to explain to their partner how they are feeling at this moment through the use of mime. Once they have performed their mime and tried to communicate in this way the partner is required to guess the feeling. Both the students should have a go at miming and guessing!

Questions for Circle Time

During this part of the session the students can focus upon the following questions:

- When did you last experience a conflict?
- How did you deal with your conflict?
- What kinds of conflicts have we observed outside of the school context?

Identify a conflict that causes you to feel aggressive, assertive or passive.

What is the conflict that most worries you at the moment (personal or public)?

Activity 1 – Feeling in conflict

This is an individual activity in which each student is required to identify the sources of the conflict they may currently be experiencing. The grid provides the students with an easy means of recording their ideas and there are blank columns and rows (three of each) in order to encourage them to do so. The students are finally required to identify the three most significant conflicts that they would most like to sort out.

Activity 2 – Key conflict

This is a stop, think, analyse activity which encourages the students to problem-solve one of the three most significant conflicts identified in the first activity. The students are also encouraged to identify how this conflict makes them feel (for example sad, upset, scared, fed up, ashamed, depressed, stressed, confused) whilst also identifying the other person involved in the conflict and attempting to identify how he or she probably feels. The next step in this problem-solving process requires the students to clarify what they want and what they think the other person wants and then to identify what they might do about this conflict and to clarify what the other person might do about this conflict. Finally, the students are asked to identify three things that they could do right at this moment in order to improve this conflict situation. This process adopts a solution focused philosophy and reinforces the importance of looking for and identifying solutions via a stepped approach to problem-solving.

Activity 3 – Conflict Information Sheet

This activity sheet provides a great deal of information and it will be helpful for the facilitator to discuss this with the class as a whole prior to asking the students to identify their own top tips for solving conflicts. This information sheet clarifies the three possible results of a conflict.

Win win, win lose and lose lose.

In a win win situation the people involved will sort out the problem without aggression, nobody will get hurt and ultimately a compromise will be found where both people can maintain their self-respect and respect for each other.

In the win lose result one person will generally use aggression in order to ensure that the other person gives in and obviously someone will get hurt whilst another person will get their own way. Ultimately both people will disrespect themselves and each other.

In a lose lose situation both people will resort to aggressive behaviours and there may be physical and emotional hurt for all concerned. Things will always end up worse than they originally were and both people will tend to disrespect themselves and each other. Ultimately nobody will be a winner in this situation.

The students are then presented with seven top tips for resolving conflicts and required to brainstorm their own top tips either with a partner or in a small group. Top tips include: listening, taking turns to talk, getting some help, compromising, waiting, problem-solving and the use of 'I' messages.

When the students have time to discuss and share their ideas in a group it may be helpful for the facilitator to highlight the usefulness and importance of each of these strategies.

Take Home Task – Problem-solving format

This activity presents the students with a format to try and solve a conflict or problem situation either at home or in the school context. This six stepped approach reinforces the importance of self-reflection, articulating the problem, clarifying options and identifying the advantages and disadvantages of possible solutions. Most importantly the final step reinforces the need to have another go should the chosen solution not be entirely appropriate or successful. Maintaining motivation and a positive attitude is what really helps in attempting to solve problems and reduce conflicts and confrontations.

Plenary

The brainstorming approach can be used in order to address the following questions:

- What have we learnt about this particular feeling?
- What have we learnt about how we experience this feeling?
- Have we learnt about how others experience this feeling?
- Are there any new concepts that we have learnt?
- Are there any new skills that we have been able to identify?
- How will this session impact upon us now and in the future?

Feeling in Conflict

Identify the sources of the conflicts you may currently be experiencing. Use the following tick system:

3 ticks = a conflict that causes you to feel very upset.
2 ticks = a conflict that causes you to feel quite upset.
1 tick = a conflict that causes you to feel a minor upset.

Record your ideas in the GRID and add in any of your own choice.

	Parents	Siblings	Boy or girlfriend	Friends	Teachers	Neighbours						
Attitudes												
Language												
Politics												
Clothes												
Your future												
Money												
Housework												
Religion												
Appearance												
School												
Homework												

Stop and think! Identify the three most significant conflicts that you'd like to sort out.

1. ____________________

2. ____________________

3. ____________________

Key Conflict

Think! Analyse! Reflect!

Problem-solve! Complete the sheet and move forwards!

A conflict I'd like to sort out is:	The other person involved is:
This conflict makes me feel (tick against feeling): sad, depressed, worried upset, stressed, confused scared, rejected, sad fed-up, frustrated, angry ashamed, disappointed, surprised	The other person probably feels (tick against feeling): sad, depressed, worried upset, stressed, confused scared, rejected, sad fed up, frustrated, angry ashamed, disappointed, surprised
What I want is:	What the other person wants is:
What I might do about this conflict is:	What the other person might do about this conflict is:

Three things I could do now to improve this situation:

1.
2.
3.

Conflict Information Sheet

There are three possible results of a conflict:

Win Win

The people involved will sort out the problem without any aggression.
Nobody gets hurt.
A compromise is found.
Both people respect themselves and each other.

Win Lose

One person uses aggression or one person gives in.
One person will get hurt.
One person will get their own way.
Both people disrespect themselves and each other.

Lose Lose

Both people will resort to aggression.
There is physical and emotional hurt for all concerned.
Things end up worse than they originally were.
Both people disrespect themselves and each other.
Nobody is a winner.

Top tips for solving conflicts

Can you add any of your own?

- Listen
- Take turns to talk
- Get some help
- Compromise
- Wait
- Problem-solve
- Use 'I' messages.

Share your ideas in a group. Do you agree with others' views? If so, why?

Take Home Task

Problem-solving Format

Use the format to try and solve a problem situation either at home or at school.

Remember: collect the information, communicate and co-operate in order to achieve a win win situation.

Step 1: What is the problem and who is involved?

Step 2: Do I need to get help? Who can I ask?

Step 3: What are the options?

Step 4: Identify solutions	Advantages	Disadvantages

Step 5: Which solution have you chosen and why?

Step 6: Try it out! If it doesn't work, have another go!

Go for it!

Session 12

Feeling Co-operative

Introduction

This session focuses on the importance of both feeling and being co-operative and the ways in which such behaviour can aid personal emotional wellbeing and ensure that others feel both comfortable and safe. The students are asked to engage in a range of co-operation skills tasks which require them to appropriately and effectively work with and alongside each other. The final self-reflection quiz encourages them to identify ways in which they may become more co-operative in specific situations that they currently find quite difficult. The facilitator can elicit the students' definitions and record these on the whiteboard or flip-chart after initially providing them with the following definition as follows:

Feeling co-operative is when you know you can get on well with others, work as a team, share and work well together.

Icebreaker

This icebreaker is entitled 'Co-operate!' The facilitator should ask the students to stand in a line in age order without speaking and check that they've got this right. Then, time allowing, the students can be asked to stand in alphabetical order of surname and the facilitator can check and reinforce that in order to complete both tasks successfully the students have been 'co-operating'!

Questions for Circle Time

At this part of the session the students can focus upon the following questions:

- What do we mean by co-operating?
- Give an example of a situation where you have co-operated well.
- Give an example of a situation where someone has not co-operated with you.
- How did you feel in both situations?
- Try to remember a situation where you observed people not co-operating with each other.
- How did this make you feel?
- How did you think the people involved felt at the time?

Activity 1 – Feeling Co-operative

This brainstorming activity requires the students to work in small groups and to share ideas and record them on the sheet provided. The question posed is: Why and when do we need to feel and be co-operative? The students will come up with a range of ideas and it may be helpful to point out similarities and differences in their responses during a small feedback time at the end of this activity. This will also encourage the students to feedback on their own discussions as to what would happen if people didn't feel co-operative.

Activity 2 – The Treasure Map

The students can participate in this activity in groups of four to five (as appropriate to the size of group). Each group is provided with a treasure map, a set of translation cards and a direction sheet. However, the translation cards are shuffled up and distributed by the facilitator so that each group only has one set of eight cards. This will mean that in order to complete the activity, i.e. translate the direction sheet in order to find treasure on the map, the students from each group will be required to co-operate and negotiate with each other in order to swap translation cards or provide each other with support. The students should start from the 'X' marked on the map. The facilitator will need to be observant to ensure that the students really do utilise their skills of co-operation and that no one in the group or class becomes frustrated or distressed during this activity. The idea is for it to be fun whilst also reinforcing the importance of developing these skills. They should find the treasure in square D7.

Activity 3 – Co-operation skills tasks

These three tasks encourage the students to develop and utilise their current skills of co-operation and negotiation. The students will need to be divided into groups of four to six and each group will be presented with one of these cards. The first card requires the students to make a structure using only pins and straws. The second card requires the class to agree on a rank order for items required subsequent to a plane crashing in the desert. The third card requires the students to decide on how they will cope subsequent to arriving in France for a camping holiday and observing the teacher collapsing with an unusual stomach bug and being rushed to hospital. All these tasks are designed to be fun and non-threatening. It may be helpful for the facilitator to point out that there is no 'right' solution or answer to each of these tasks and the importance is placed upon the students co-operating and developing their skills in the process.

Take Home Task Self-reflection quiz

This activity requires the students to reflect upon their own skills. The students are asked to identify when they are most co-operative and why this is the case, i.e. who helps them and how they help themselves in such situations. They are then asked to identify when they feel like not co-operating and why this should be the case, i.e. what is it that makes it so difficult for them? Finally, they are asked to identify one situation or time when they found it the most difficult to co-operate and to then record their reasons and identify the things that they may be able to do in order to increase their co-operation in this situation. Once again the emphasis here is upon remaining solution focused and maintaining a positive attitude. There is also a focus on responsibility and remaining in control of both behaviour and the context.

Plenary

The brainstorming approach can be used in order to address the following questions:

- What have we learnt about this particular feeling?
- What have we learnt about how we experience this feeling?
- Have we learnt about how others experience this feeling?
- Are there any new concepts that we have learnt?
- Are there any new skills that we have been able to identify?
- How will this session impact upon us now and in the future?

Feeling Co-operative

Brainstorming activity! Work in small groups and share your ideas, recording them on this sheet.

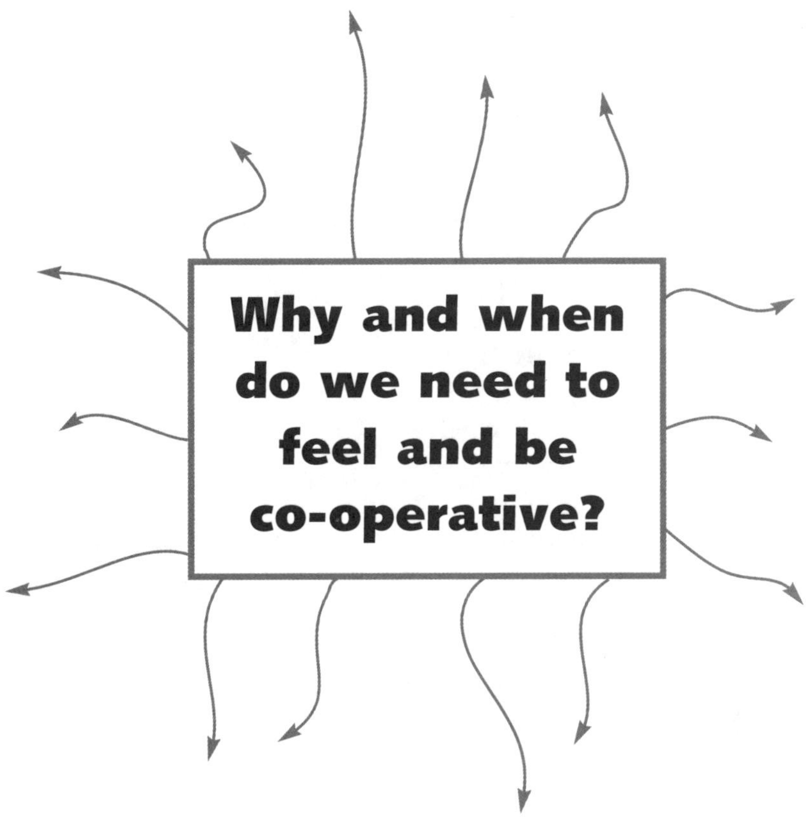

Stop and reflect! What do you think would happen if people did not feel co-operative during the following:

A football match

At the supermarket checkout

A game of cards.

The Treasure Map

Find your fortune!

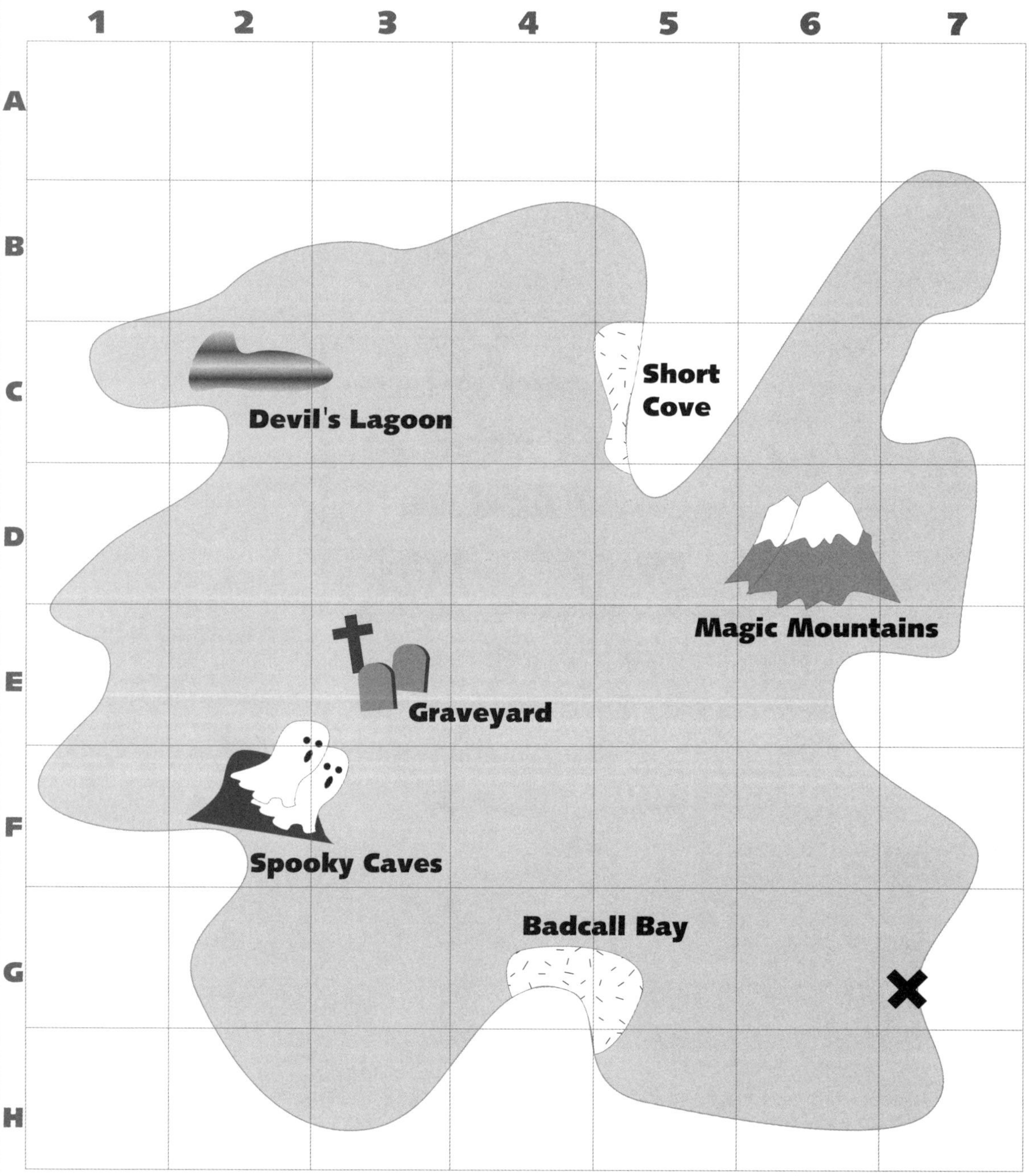

Translation Cards

Left – NOTIL	Five – DURMA	Instructions – MAZZ
Right – SURBUL	Six – PISAL	To – SOP
Up – EPPI	Crack – COBT	Find – AFT
Down – FOGUL	This – MEGAN	Treasure – ORETON
One – SEPO	Code – SOLOPP	Go – PEBO
Two – CHAN	And – PATRUN	For – WAK
Three – ORTO.	Follow – MAGOON	It – FROCH
Four – FELG	The – FILIPT	Now – POLOZ

Direction Sheet

COBT MEGAN SOLOPP PATRUN MAGOON FILIPT MAZZ SOP AFT FILIPT ORETON.

PEBO WAK FROCH POLOZ!

Notil Durma
Eppi Felg
Surbul Orto
Surbul Chan
Fogul Durma
Eppi Pisal
Notil Sepo
Durma Fogul
Chan Notil
Eppi Chan
Notil Sepo
Chan Eppi
Orto surbul
Sepo fogul
Sepo Surbul.

Co-operation Skills Tasks

Make a structure

Materials: Lots of pins and straws Time: 10-15 minutes Group: 4-6

You have between 10-15 minutes to build a structure. You can only use pins and straws. When you have finished, the structure will be assessed for its stability, height and unique shape.

Before you start, discuss how you will achieve this objective and how each member of the group can play an active part.

Survive the Desert

Materials: Pen and paper Time: 10-15 minutes Group: 4-6

Your plane has crash landed in the desert and your group are the only survivors. It is 100F already and there is only desert and sand around you. Which are the most important for your survival? Agree a rank order for the following items:

Gun (loaded)	A parachute	A mirror
Torch	Powdered milk	A litre of milk
Bottle of salt tablets	A compass	A pen knife

Carry on Camping

Materials: Pen and paper Time: 10-15 minutes Group 4-6

You have just arrived in the South of France for a camping holiday when your teacher collapses with an unusual stomach bug and is rushed to hospital. Your group decides to go ahead with the holiday. All your equipment such as tents, blow-up beds and cookers needs to be unpacked and the campsite shop closes in 20 minutes. There are no shops for 20 miles and nobody to drive the minibus. You need to decide on:

The jobs that need to be done

Who will do them

Special outings for both the day and evening for one week

Take Home Task

Self-reflection Quiz

Stop and think! Read the questions and try to answer them as honestly as you can. Try to identify ways that you can become more co-operative in specific situations.

When are you most co-operative? (Think of the main situations.)

____

____

Why? What or who helps you and how do you help yourself?

____

____

____

When do you feel like not co-operating?

____

____

Why? What is it that makes it difficult for you? Think of your attitudes and those of others?

____

____

Identify one situation or time when you found it hardest to co-operate. Record your reasons and identify the things that you can do to increase your co-operation in the table below.

Situation	Reasons for difficulties	Ways forward (identify strategies and others who may be able to help)

Try out your strategies and ideas. Go for it!

Session 13

Feeling Empathic

Introduction

In this session the students are encouraged to formulate their definitions of empathy and to articulate how and when they experience this feeling state. They are encouraged also to distinguish between empathy and sympathy in order to avoid confusing the two feelings. Developing the ability to empathise with others is also focused on in the activities which include analysing how others are feeling and attempting to identify and articulate the feelings of significant others. The students are also encouraged to empathise with others in the problem-solving process and to recognise how solutions will generally be easier to construct when there is real empathy between the problem-solver and the person with the problem.

The facilitator can elicit the students' definitions as to the nature of empathy on the whiteboard or flip-chart after initially providing the following definition.

Feeling empathic is when you are able to put yourself in someone else's shoes and really feel what they are feeling.

Icebreaker

This icebreaker activity is entitled 'Positive Points'. Each student has a piece of paper taped onto his or her back and the other students in the group should then write positive comments about this particular student on the piece of paper. The bigger the group the greater the length of time will be needed in order to successfully complete this activity. However, the students are only required to write down one word or one short phrase for each member of their peer group. At the end of the activity the pieces of paper can be removed and the students will be able to read through the positive points made by others about them.

Questions for Circle Time

During this part of the session the students can focus upon the following questions:

- When have you felt sorry for somebody?
- When have you felt as though you really understood how someone else was feeling?
- Have you ever felt that someone else really understood how you were feeling?
- Why do you think it's important for people to be able to empathise with others?
- What would happen if people couldn't read others' feelings and didn't empathise with them?

Activity 1 – Feeling Empathic

This brainstorming activity encourages the students to produce their personal definitions for empathy and to also articulate and analyse times when they have experienced this feeling state. The students are further required to discuss the importance of not confusing empathy with sympathy. It may be helpful, therefore, for the activity itself to be conducted in pairs so as to encourage discussion.

Activity 2 – Put Yourself in my Shoes

The sixteen themes provided on the four handouts can be read through by the students in a small group. They can then be given the opportunity to discuss how each character in each scene feels and to provide their reasons for making such an assessment.

It may helpful for the course facilitator to have photocopied these onto A4 card prior to the start of the session and perhaps laminated and cut out the scene cards. It may also be useful to provide four scenes per group rather than expect the students to read through and complete their discussion around all sixteen scenes. However, this can be left to the discretion of the facilitator.

Activity 3 – Developing Empathy, Problem-solving

In this activity the students are required to take on the role of an agony aunt or uncle by reading through three problem cards, empathising with the character portrayed in each card and attempting to construct a useful and helpful response for each problem. Finally, there is a self-reflection activity where the students are asked to consider someone who has recently empathised with them and to identify how this may have helped them.

Take Home Task – Feelings quiz – how do they feel?

This activity requires the students to consider and observe some significant people in their lives and to attempt to identify when and why they would be experiencing the following feelings:

- happiness
- sadness
- fear
- anger
- embarrassment.

They are asked to observe their parents or carer, best friend, form tutor, sister, brother or cousin and one other person and to then check out with these people how accurate their observations may or may not have been. Finally, once the students have clarified the accuracy of their observations, they are also required to consider how they might further develop their skills of empathy.

Plenary

The brainstorming approach can be used in order to address the following questions:

- What have we learnt about this particular feeling?
- What have we learnt about how we experience this feeling?
- Have we learnt about how others experience this feeling?
- Are there any new concepts that we have learnt?
- Are there any new skills that we have been able to identify?
- How will this session impact upon us now and in the future?

Feeling Empathic

What is empathy? When do we know we experience this feeling state? What do we do? Record your definitions on this brainstorming chart.

Remember!

Empathy is not to be confused with sympathy. Discuss this statement with a partner and try to identify the differences.

Put Yourself in My Shoes

Scene 1

Janice was waiting for the bus. It was freezing cold and the snow was just beginning to fall. Suddenly she heard someone shouting and laughing down the road. When she looked up she saw a group of boys coming towards her. They were making a lot of noises and pushing each other.

How do you think she feels?

Scene 2

Mrs Edmunds went into the classroom and asked the students to settle down and listen. She placed all her handouts and notes on the table at the front of the room. Two boys walked up to the table and pushed one pile onto the floor.

How do you think she feels?

Scene 3

Alfie went outside and sat down on the side of the road. How could his Mum have walked out on them? Perhaps if he phoned and begged her, she might come back to live with them. Or maybe she wouldn't.

How do you think he feels?

Scene 4

All of Joseph's friends had been picked for the football team. They were due to go over to Rouen in France to play with their 'twinned' school. Joseph knew that he was just as good a player as all of his friends. He couldn't understand it.

How do you think he feels?

Put Yourself in My Shoes

Scene 5

Josh walked into the playground and saw them waiting. There were six of them now and just as they saw him they all crowded round him. One boy called him a fat slob and started to punch him in the arm.

How do you think he feels?

Scene 6

Jane's Mum died of lung cancer last year and her Dad was really upset when he found out that Jane had started to smoke. He made her promise to give up and she said she had. However, he then saw her smoking a cigarette in the park last Friday.

How do you think Jane's dad feels?

How do you think Jane feels?

Scene 7

Jane had been going out with Mike for three months. He was really good looking and secretly Jane didn't understand why he fancied her. Then, last week, Mike didn't turn up for their evening out at the cinema. The next day she saw that he had two love bites on his neck.

How do you think Jane feels?

How do you think Mike feels?

Scene 8

Simon saw the two boys go into the shop and thought he recognised them but he wasn't absolutely certain. He walked in behind them and saw them stealing some t-shirts from behind the counter. They brushed past him as they ran out and one of them said, "Split and you're dead meat."

How do you think Simon feels?

How do you think the two boys feel?

Put Yourself in My Shoes

Scene 9

Carla was always thought to be a real boffin by other members of her form group. Throughout Year 7, she'd got top grades in all her subjects and was always being asked to display her work. Last year the English teacher used her essay on The Tempest as a model of excellence for Year 11 students. However, yesterday she got the results back from the KS3 SATS and she scored really badly on her science paper.

How do you think she feels?

Scene 10

Adil's Dad has been a school governor for the past three years and has always supported the school. He regularly financed the football team's kit and attended every match. He felt strongly that he should support the team as Adil was the goalie. However, Adil got himself excluded from the team last Thursday because he made a racist comment to another boy.

How do you think Adil feels?

How do you think his dad feels?

Scene 11

Jake's best friends have stopped talking to him because he refused to smoke a joint with them at Hayley's birthday party. They said he was dumb and living in the dark ages. Jake doesn't want to feel or be labelled as uncool but he just doesn't want to smoke the stuff.

How do you think he feels?

Scene 12

Janine's Mum and Dad are splitting up because her Mum has been being having an affair with their next door neighbour, Ted. She's now decided to move in with him and Janine is going to stay with her dad. It is tricky because Janine's best friend is Ted's daughter and now she won't speak to Janine because she feels so angry about the situation.

How do you think Janine feels?

Put Yourself in My Shoes

Scene 13

Mrs Smith lives at Number 28 and she is very old and frail. Lately, she's been bothered by a gang of girls who continually shout at her in the street and throw stones at her windows. They call her 'the old witch' and accuse her of practising black magic. Last week they got hold of her cat and set its tail alight. Mrs Smith called the police but they said there was nothing they could do as there were no witnesses to the crime.

How do you think she feels?

How do you think the members of the gang feel?

Scene 14

Mr Orfanau couldn't believe his eyes. The whole form room was absolutely wrecked. There was graffiti all over the walls and doors and all the plants had been uprooted and thrown out of the windows. Worst of all, someone had obviously urinated in the corner. He couldn't understand it. How could anyone do this when his Year 6 group had worked so hard?

How do you think he feels?

Scene 15

Hala looked quite stunned when she walked into the classroom. She had only been in England for three weeks and never been to school before now. She waited as everyone appeared to be writing and wondered if she'd eventually be able to write as well. She looked carefully at the form tutor who was smiling at her and directing her to a seat at the front of the class. She didn't understand a word that was being spoken apart from 'hello'.

How do you think she feels?

Scene 16

Hannah's Dad died last August. It was all very sudden. He had a heart attack, fell down the stairs and died within 25 minutes. Hannah was at school when this happened and was called to the hospital after the event. She was shocked of course but also distressed as she'd had a huge argument with her Dad the night before he died and said that she wished he were dead.

How do you think she feels?

Feelings Quiz
How do they feel?

Look Understand Listen Talk Reflect Empathise

Think about and observe some significant people in your life and try to identify when and why they experience these feelings.

Complete the chart.

Person	Happiness	Fear	Excitement	Anger	Embarrassment	Sadness
Parent or carer	When? Why?	When? Why?	When? Why?	When? Why?	When? Why?	When? Why?
Best friend	When? Why?	When? Why?	When? Why?	When? Why?	When? Why?	When? Why?
Form tutor	When? Why?	When? Why?	When? Why?	When? Why?	When? Why?	When? Why?
Sister/ brother/cousin	When? Why?	When? Why?	When? Why?	When? Why?	When? Why?	When? Why?
Other	When? Why?	When? Why?	When? Why?	When? Why?	When? Why?	When? Why?

Check it out! Ask one of these people how accurate your observations are. Are you as empathic as you thought? Do you find it easy to put yourself in someone else's shoes? If not, how might you develop this skill?

Take Home Activity

Developing empathy
Problem-solving

Look at the three problem cards below. Can you emphasise with each individual and complete the response cards?

1. Problem	2. Problem	3. Problem
Emma has a maths test on Friday. She hasn't revised at all because she thinks she's rubbish at maths and it won't be worth it. She came bottom in the last test and everyone made fun of her and called her dumb.	Kevin's girlfriend has just split with him and started going out with his best friend. They are now making a big thing about being a couple and keep sitting in front of him in class, holding hands and kissing each other whenever they can.	Haja's parents are strict Muslims. They won't let her go out on her own in the evening and would never let her mix with boys at a disco or club. She isn't even allowed round to her girlfriend's house because the family aren't Muslim.
1. Response How does she feel? What could you say and do? How can you empathise?	2. Response How does he feel? What could you say and do? How can you empathise?	3. Response How does she feel? What could you say and do? How could you empathise?

Stop and Think!

Who has recently empathised with you? How did this help you? Were you able to move on in any way?

Session 14

Feeling Different

Introduction

This session introduces the notion of difference and the students are asked to consider when and why feeling different is not always a comfortable experience. The concept of alienation is considered and the reasons why people may or may not feel alienated in society are also highlighted. The students are given the opportunity to consider why feeling different can also be a positive experience, i.e. when someone wants to or enjoys standing out from the crowd. There is a focus upon developing and utilising empathy and the students are given the opportunity to consider a range of bullying related problems and to brainstorm some useful and constructive solutions and advice. Finally, there is the opportunity for each student in the class to celebrate their own uniqueness and difference.

The facilitator can elicit the students' views and definitions of difference and provide the following initial definition:

Feeling different is when you know that you are different from other people and this can make you feel alienated or proud. It can consequently be either a comfortable or an uncomfortable experience.

Icebreaker

This icebreaker is entitled 'Draw It'. One student is volunteered to stand with his or her back to the class and to describe a picture that he or she has drawn. This can be fairly simple and composed of some geometric shapes. The student is able to describe this in words only whilst the class reproduce this on individual sheets of paper. Once the students have reproduced this picture the student at the front of the class can turn round and encourage the students in the class to compare their own drawings. The same activity can then be repeated with the volunteer student facing the class and using his or her hands as well as words in order to describe the shape. The students can then have a second go at reproducing the shape and compare both drawings. The idea here is to reinforce the importance of communicating effectively and the ways in which we make use of both verbal and non-verbal skills when communicating with others.

Questions for Circle Time

During this part of the session the students can focus upon the following questions:

- When do we feel different?
- When do we recognise others as being different?
- Are people frightened of differences? If so, why?
- How do we behave when we meet someone who is very different to ourselves?
- How do you think you would feel if you had to go to a new school where nobody spoke your language or looked the same as you?

Activity 1 – Feeling Different

This brainstorming activity encourages the students to ask the question, "When and why do we feel different?" The students are asked to consider both positive and negative aspects of feeling different and to then analyse any agreement on whether feeling different is generally a comfortable or an uncomfortable feeling.

Activity 2 – Different Strokes

In this activity, the students are required to describe two imaginary people, one that they would really like to be and one that they wouldn't like to be. After recording descriptions on 'people postcards' they are asked to consider a series of questions. This process involves identifying why they would prefer to be one person as opposed to the other and how they think they would be treated if they were either of these people. They are also introduced to the concept of change and asked to identify the kinds of changes they may or may not experience if they were to turn into someone else.

Activity 3 – Bully box, dealing with difference

In this activity the students are required to consider five notes which detail a variety of bullying incidents experienced by young people in schools. The problem-solving format from Session 10 (Who? Me?) can be used here as a framework for the students to record their responses to each of these problems. It is probably easiest for the students to work in pairs in order to reinforce the importance of developing joint problem-solving skills and to particularly make use of stepped approaches to solving difficult problems. This is another opportunity for the students to also develop empathy.

Take Home Task – You are unique, celebrate the difference!

This self-esteem building exercise reinforces the fact that every individual is different, special and unique. Nobody in the world is exactly the same as anyone else with the same thoughts, ideas, feelings, behaviours, dreams, words, fears and fantasies and appearance. This is what makes us all special and all different. This self-reflection activity requires the students to focus upon their own uniqueness.

Finally, the students are asked to consider things about their unique selves that they may like to change in the future. They are asked to identify one or two such changes and to then work out how they might effect them and who would help and support them in order to achieve the best outcome.

Plenary

The brainstorming approach can be used in order to address the following questions:

- What have we learnt about this particular feeling?
- What have we learnt about how we experience this feeling?
- Have we learnt about how others experience this feeling?
- Are there any new concepts that we have learnt?
- Are there any new skills that we have been able to identify?
- How will this session impact upon us now and in the future?

Feeling Different

Feeling different is not always a comfortable experience. Sometimes it can cause you to feel alienated from the group. However, sometimes it is a more positive experience and we like to feel different and stand out from the crowd. Work in a small group and discuss your thoughts on this topic prior to completing the brainstorming activity.

Is there any agreement as to whether or not feeling different is generally a comfortable or uncomfortable feeling? If so, why? If not, why not?

Different Strokes

Describe two 'imaginary' people – one that you would really like to be and one who you wouldn't like to be. Use the 'people postcards' below.

Name: ____________	Photo	Name: ____________	Photo
Gender: ____________		Gender: ____________	
Race ____________		Race ____________	
Hair colour ____________		Hair colour ____________	
Eye colour ____________		Eye colour ____________	
Height ____________		Height ____________	
Weight ____________		Weight ____________	
Likes and dislikes ____________		Likes and dislikes ____________	
Talents ____________		Talents ____________	
Friends ____________		Friends ____________	
Hobbies ____________		Hobbies ____________	

Now consider the following questions:

- Why would you prefer to be person A?
- How would your life be different if you were person B?
- How do you think other people would treat person A and person B? What would be the differences and why?
- If you could be person A now, how would your life be better? What changes would you experience?

Bully Box

Dealing with Difference

The following notes were found in one secondary school's Bully Box. Use the problem-solving format from Session 10 as a framework for your responses to each problem. Work in groups and try to give some useful and constructive advice to each pupil.

I am being bullied because I am fat. I can't lose weight. I starve myself and then binge eat because I feel so fed up. Four girls in my form keep thumping, pinching and kicking me and calling me names. They are all slim and pretty and popular with the boys. Please help.

I am being bullied by three racists in my class. They keep on calling me 'gorilla features' because I am African and they tease me about my accent. I am at risk of really losing it and thumping them because I feel so angry, but I don't want to as I know it will upset my Dad and he'll hit me with the belt.

I'm being bullied by my big brother. I know that he is having sex with his girlfriend because I walked in on them. He's 14 and I know he shouldn't have sex until he's 16. Now he continually pushes and shoves me and says that if I tell he'll strangle my dog. I think he'll do this because he's quite violent and has hit me a lot in the past.

I am being bullied by my Stepmum. I know she didn't like me from the start because I'm tall and clumsy and I keep breaking stuff by accident. She says I should be neat like her two girls but I think they're creeps. She's started to say that I've broken things when I haven't to get me into trouble with Dad. I think it's so she can send me to my real Mum and get rid of me.

I am being bullied by my English teacher. It's not just me. There are four of us in the class and I think it's because we all find writing hard and we're no good at spelling. I can't copy from the board and he rubs it off before I've finished and then I can't do the homework because I don't know what it is. He's also said nasty things when I try to read aloud and even laughs if I have a go. I feel like giving up totally. I know I'm not good at the subject but he doesn't need to make me feel like a total idiot.

Take Home Task

You are Unique!

Celebrate the Difference!

In all the world, there is nobody quite like you! There are people who are different and people who are similar but nobody is exactly the same, with the same thoughts, ideas, feelings, behaviours, dreams, words, hopes, fantasies and appearance. Stop for a time and reflect upon these areas – jot down some notes in each box.

A unique thought	A unique feeling	A unique fear

A unique hope	A unique fantasy	A unique dream

A unique appearance	A unique word or statement	A unique idea

There may be some things that you'd like to change in the future. Try to identify one or two of these and then work out how you might effect such a change and who will help and support you in doing this.

Session 15

Feeling Reflective

Introduction

The skills of self-reflection and the ability to reflect upon situations and life events are crucial to developing one's level of Emotional Literacy. Consequently, this session both introduces and reinforces the central theme to the whole programme. The students are provided with an opportunity to reflect upon themselves and their own achievements whilst also gaining a further understanding as to how it is possible to learn from their mistakes. The key skill of motivation and the importance of positive thinking is reinforced. The students also have the opportunity to undertake an Emotional Literacy self-reflection exercise in order to address any current unhelpful or negative behaviours. They are finally required to consider how they experienced three key emotions at various stages of their lives, for example 5-6 years, 9-10 years and at their current age. This activity is intended to reinforce how levels of Emotional Literacy develop through time and how everyone can further develop their ability to manage uncomfortable feelings and capitalise on those which are generally more comfortable.

The facilitator can elicit the students' definitions regarding feeling reflective and provide the initial definition:

Feeling reflective is when you can stop and think about yourself and things you have done and consider why you might do things differently next time.

Icebreaker

This icebreaker activity is entitled 'Spin It!' The facilitator spins an empty bottle in the middle of a circle. When it stops, the person sitting opposite it has to speak on the topic of 'how I feel today and why I feel...today'. This person then has the next spin. The students may proceed to speak on the topic of 'how I felt yesterday and why I felt... yesterday'.

Questions for Circle Time

During this part of the session the students can focus upon the following questions:

- What do we mean when we use the word reflection?
- Why is it important to think about what we have said and done in the past?
- Can we learn from previous experiences?
- When have you done something in the past that you know you will do differently next time?
- What is your most positive memory or experience to date?
- Can you describe the mistakes that you made that you know you have learnt from?

Activity 1 – Reflection

This initial brainstorming activity requires the students to stop, think and reflect upon themselves, their achievements and the skills that they have learnt to date. The students are required to record their ideas around a 'self-portrait mirror'. Further reflection and analysis of one achievement is then encouraged. The aim here is to encourage the students to also consider how they can learn from previous experience in order to effect more positive changes and outcomes in the future.

Activity 2 – Learn from Your Mistakes

This is an extremely important concept as many of us tend to feel down when we know that we have made a mistake or done something wrong. However, it is important to note that by making mistakes we can actually learn and change and develop in the future. The students are asked to stop, think and reflect in order to identify one mistake that they have made in the past and identify the outcomes for both themselves and any other people involved. They are then required to think back and reflect on what they could have done in order to have achieved a better outcome. This solution focused approach, encourages the students to turn negatives into positives and to see life as a learning process rather than something they need to 'get right' all the time.

Activity 3 – Emotional Literacy: self-reflection exercise

This exercise specifically focuses upon raising the students' awareness as to their level of Emotional Literacy and is the kind of self-reflection exercise that they can utilise on a regular basis. The students are asked to identify four main feelings that they are most likely to experience in a school day and to then describe how they may behave or act when experiencing these feelings. The final part of the activity requires them to think carefully about any unhelpful or negative behaviours and to identify what is happening and why. This is not an easy thing to do and sufficient time should be allocated alongside providing the students with the opportunity to discuss this with a partner. This seven stepped self-reflection process also encourages the students to visualise how they would like things to be different in this particular situation and to then articulate how they would be able to make this happen and to identify possible sources of support for this process. This is a solution focused problem-solving activity and the key to its success is the level of honest self-reflection that the student is willing to engage in.

Take Home Task – Major memories

This activity requires the students to reflect upon how they experienced the feelings of anger, stress and excitement at the ages of 5-6, 9-10 and at their current age. They are then required to consider the differences between each of these responses at these specific ages. Do they experience these feelings differently and if so why do they think this is the case? The focus here is on identifying and articulating the students' current level of skills in managing uncomfortable feelings more effectively.

Plenary

The brainstorming approach can be used in order to address the following questions:

- What have we learnt about this particular feeling?
- What have we learnt about how we experience this feeling?
- Have we learnt about how others experience this feeling?
- Are there any new concepts that we have learnt?
- Are there any new skills that we have been able to identify?
- How will this session impact upon us now and in the future?

Reflection

Look into the mirror and draw what you see. Then stop and think! Reflect upon yourself, your achievements and the skills that you have learnt to date. Record your ideas around the mirror.

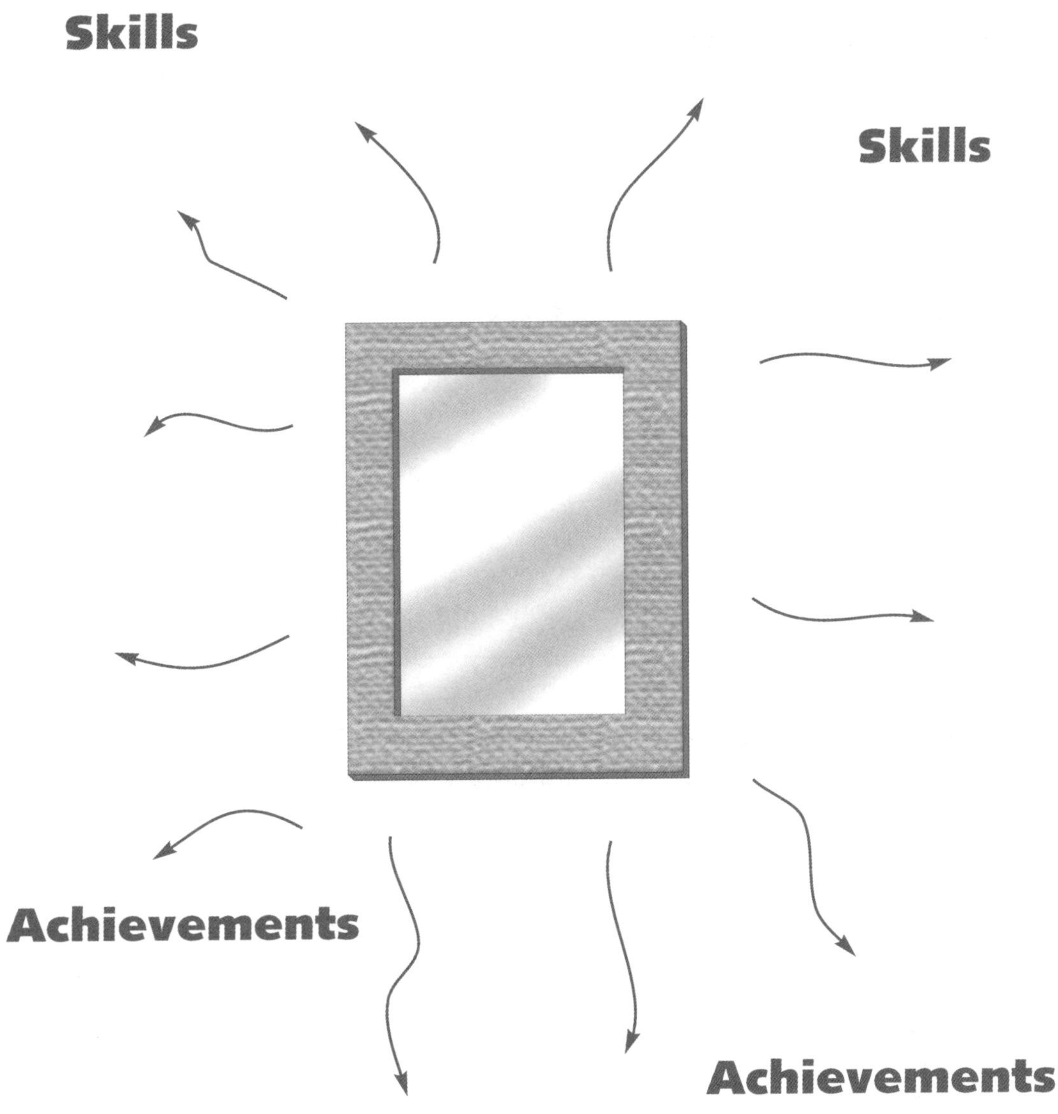

Now consider one achievement in detail and answer the following questions on the reverse of this sheet:

Why did you achieve this?

What did you feel, think and do at the time?

Would you do anything differently in a similar situation in the future?

Learn from Your Mistakes

Everyone makes mistakes – that's how we learn! Stop, think and reflect. Identify one mistake that you have made in the past and the outcomes for you and any other people involved.

My mistake – what happened?

Now think back and reflect again. What would have achieved a better outcome? What would you have done, felt and said differently?

A better outcome – what would be different?

Emotional Literacy Self-Reflection Exercise

Step 1: Draw and label the four main feelings you are most likely to experience in a school day.

Feeling 1 ____________ Feeling 2 ____________ Feeling 3 ____________ Feeling 4 ____________

Step 2: How do you behave when you experience each of these feelings?

Feeling 1: I ________________________________

Feeling 2: I ________________________________

Feeling 3: I ________________________________

Feeling 4: I ________________________________

Step 3: Think about any unhelpful or negative behaviours. What is happening and why? (This is quite difficult, so take your time.)

Emotional Literacy Self-Reflection Exercise

Step 4: Now think about how you would like things to be different.

I would like

____

____

____

Step 5: What can you do to make this happen?

Step 6 : What can other people do to make this happen?

Step 7: How will you feel if this does happen? What will be different for you?

Try it out! Go for it!

Take Home Task

Major Memories

Stop, think and reflect! Try to remember how, when and why you experienced the following feelings at the ages of 5-6 and 9-10 years and then identify how, when and why you experience the feelings now. Record your ideas in the boxes.

Anger

5-6 years	9-10 years	Now

Stress

5-6 years	9-10 years	Now

Excitement

5-6 years	9-10 years	Now

Now consider the differences. How have you changed? Do you experience these feelings differently? Are the causes now different? Have you developed in your ability to manage the uncomfortable more effectively? Discuss your ideas and current strategies with a friend.

Session 16

Feeling Friendly

Introduction

This session focuses upon identifying the characteristics, behaviours and skills of a friend alongside reinforcing the importance of empathy in developing and maintaining positive relationships. The students are given the opportunity to analyse their own skills in this area and to consider ways in which they may be able to further develop their skills.

The facilitator can elicit the students' own definitions as to feeling friendly and provide an additional prompt as follows:

Feeling friendly is when you feel empathy, kindness and loyalty to others and are willing to show it.

Icebreaker

This icebreaker activity is entitled 'Mirror Movements'. Each student is required to identify a partner and stand opposite him or her. Both the students are then required to imagine that there is a mirror between them and to move extremely slowly – one person adopting the role of the leader, whilst the other student attempts to mirror the leader's movements as if he or she were their reflection. The students can then swap over roles.

Questions for Circle Time

During this part of the session the students can focus upon the following questions:

- What is a friend?
- When have you been a good friend to someone?
- Who was your best friend and why?
- What is most important to you in a friend?
- Why do people need friends?
- Do you think you have been a good friend?

Activity 1 – Brainstorming – Focus on Feeling Friendly

In this activity the students are asked to work with a partner in order to share their ideas as to what constitutes a good friend. They are asked to identify the characteristics, behaviours and skills of a friend and to record their ideas on the brainstorming chart. It is important to encourage discussion in this activity and for the students to consider the notion of perfection. For example, do friends make mistakes? Should they make mistakes? Is it true that we all make mistakes? This may also involve considering the notions of forgiveness, retribution, honesty and sincerity.

Activity 2 – How Do You Feel?

This activity requires the students to work with a partner and to brainstorm their ideas. Would they really feel the same way as each other or would they feel differently in each of these situations? It will be important to allocate sufficient time so as to enable the students to have a discussion and identify ways in which they would most appropriately support a friend who found themselves in each of these situations.

Activity 3 - Friendship Quiz

This is another self-reflection activity in which the students are asked to analyse their own skills in this area. The students are required to rate themselves against fifteen friendship statements on a scale of 1-5. One being 'not a lot', three being 'OK' and five being 'always'. The final part of the activity requires the students to identify their strongest skills and those which they need to further build upon.

Take Home Task - Friendship Targets

This take home activity follows directly on from the friendship quiz self-assessment task. The students are asked to set their own personal friendship targets and to identify four ways in which they can become a better friend. They are finally asked to complete the sentence, "I will know that I have met my targets because..."

Plenary

The brainstorming approach can be used in order to address the following questions :

- What have we learnt about this particular feeling?
- What have we learnt about how we experience this feeling?
- Have we learnt about how others experience this feeling?
- Are there any new concepts that we have learnt?
- Are there any new skills that we have been able to identify?
- How will this session impact upon us now and in the future?

Brainstorming
Focus on Feeling Friendly

Work with a partner and share your ideas. What makes a good friend? What are the characteristics, behaviours and skills of a friend? Record your ideas on the chart below.

A good friend is...	**A good friend isn't...**
•	•
•	•
•	•
•	•
•	•
•	•
•	•
•	•
•	•
•	•
•	•
•	•
•	•

How Do You Feel?

How would you feel in each of these situations?

1. Somebody is following you home late at night.	2. Your Mum won't speak to you because you were late in.
3. Your sister got £500 for her birthday from her Dad whilst your Dad gave you £20.	4. You have just won the Lottery.
5. Your best friend has just been diagnosed with cancer.	6. Your form tutor has asked to see your parents/carers because you were so rude to him.
7. You can't go on the trip because you hit your friend.	8. A terrorist attack has just taken place and you have to evacuate the school buildings.
9. You came bottom in the maths test.	10. Your Nan died last week and you really loved her.
11. Three older kids are bullying you and are now waiting at the gate.	12. You've just been given the chance to go to a new school.

Work with a partner and brainstorm your ideas. Would you feel the same way or would you feel differently?

How would you support a friend in each of these situations? How would you feel and act and what would you say?

Friendship Quiz

Stop, think and reflect.
How are your friendship skills?

Rate yourself honestly! What kind of friend are you? How are your skills? Rate yourself against each statement

1 = not a lot 3 = OK 5 = always

Statement	My rating
1. I can listen properly to my friends.	1 2 3 4 5
2. I don't judge them.	1 2 3 4 5
3. I respect their views and feelings.	1 2 3 4 5
4. I am honest with them about my views and feelings.	1 2 3 4 5
5. I can tell my friends that I don't agree with them.	1 2 3 4 5
6. I don't talk about them behind their backs.	1 2 3 4 5
7. I don't put them down.	1 2 3 4 5
8. I try not to take my problems out on them.	1 2 3 4 5

Friendship Quiz

Continued

9. I can recognise and empathise with how they are feeling.	1 2 3 4 5
10. I can motivate my friends to do their best.	1 2 3 4 5
11. I can support them when they feel down.	1 2 3 4 5
12. I don't try to push my friends into doing what I want to do.	1 2 3 4 5
13. I can respect that they are different to me in some ways.	1 2 3 4 5
14. I can cope with the fact that they might need to be on their own sometimes.	1 2 3 4 5
15. I can cope with the fact that they have other friends.	1 2 3 4 5

Stop and think!

Can you be a better friend?

Where are your strongest skills?

Where do you need to improve your skills?

Complete the friendship targets take home activity and commit to being a better friend!

Take Home Task

Friendship Targets

Commit to being a better friend. Set your personal friendship targets.

I will be a better friend by:

1. ______________________________

____

2. ______________________________

____

3. ______________________________

____

4. ______________________________

I will know that I have met my targets because…

____

____

____

____

____

____

____

____

____

____

____

____

Signed ______________________________ Date ______________

Session 17

Feeling Moody

Introduction

This session encourages the students to identify why they might feel 'moody' and begin to be able to recognise triggers to specific moods in order to develop strategies to deal more effectively with these times. The activities reinforce that it is OK to have moods or mood swings and that these are frequently part of growing up and often a direct result of hormonal changes. There is also an opportunity to observe the mood swings of others and to assess when and how they may be able to support others when things get difficult. The students are also introduced to a four stepped approach to solving problems which may arise from or cause them to feel or experience mood swings. Finally, there is a focus upon turning negatives into positives and a reinforcement of the importance of being able to self-motivate and effect personal change.

The facilitator can elicit the students' personal definitions of moodiness and record these on a whiteboard or flip-chart alongside providing an initial definition as follows:

Feeling moody is when you feel uncomfortable and don't want to be around others and this can cause you to withdraw and sometimes become aggressive.

Icebreaker

This icebreaker activity is entitled 'Blank Brain'. The facilitator can introduce an activity by explaining that there are often times when we feel as if our mind has gone blank and we don't know what to say. The students are then asked to go through the following process which may be written onto a whiteboard or flip-chart in order to prompt the students.

- Think of a recent time this happened to you.
- What was the situation? Describe it.
- How would you recognise this situation next time.
- How can you prevent your mind going blank.
- What would you say next time in a similar situation?

The students can work in pairs and take it in turns to describe their own situations. This paired approach should also allow them to participate in joint problem-solving. Each pair can feedback to the group as a whole, time permitting.

Questions for Circle Time

During this part of the session the students can focus upon the following questions:

- When did you last feel moody?
- What caused your mood?
- What do you tend to do when you get into a mood?
- Is there anyone who can help you when you're in a mood?
- How do you know when your friend, parent/carer or form tutor is in a mood?
- How does their mood make you feel and behave?
- What strategies do you use in order to cope effectively with a bad mood?

Activity 1 – Feeling Moody

This activity requires the students to identify their own mood triggers and to record these on a brainstorming sheet. The sentence completion activity is as follows: "I get moody when…" The students are then required to compare their triggers with those of their friends and to discuss their responses in a smaller group. It would be helpful, therefore, if the facilitator would act as a scribe once each group has fed back their ideas as this will also allow for further analysis of responses, i.e. what are the differences and similarities? Do we tend to get into a mood for similar reasons? What are the main triggers to moodiness in this particular group?

Activity 2 – Mood Cards

This activity reinforces the importance of observing and developing empathy for others. The students are required to look carefully at those around them and to identify possible triggers to their mood swings or moods. The students are asked to complete a mood card for the people in their lives.

The students are also required to identify any similarities or differences in their triggers and to try to figure out how each individual would feel prior to getting into such a mood. Finally, they are required to consider what they may be able to do in order to help each of these individuals and to record their ideas on the reverse of the activity sheet.

Activity 3 – Manage that Mood

This activity encourages the students to utilise a problem-solving format in order to find solutions to a range of situations or events that might cause them to feel moody. It may be helpful to reinforce some of the previous strategies covered in the course such as anger and stress management strategies and problem-solving processes prior to asking the students to complete this particular activity.

This stepped process prompts the students to maintain a positive approach and to remain solution focused.

Take Home Task – Good moods

This final take home activity asks the students to make a self-contract to cope effectively with moods that they experience. The students are asked to identify eight strategies or self-talk phrases that they may use next time they are feeling moody. These are recorded in the form of a letter which the students can place in a prominent part of their bedrooms at home. It is intended to prompt them into making use of these strategies next time they experience a difficult situation which causes them to feel moody and want to isolate themselves or become aggressive toward those who they perceive to be the cause of their difficulties.

Plenary

The brainstorming approach can be used in order to address the following questions:

- What have we learnt about this particular feeling?
- What have we learnt about how we experience this feeling?
- Have we learnt about how others experience this feeling?
- Are there any new concepts that we have learnt?
- Are there any new skills that we have been able to identify?
- How will this session impact upon us now and in the future?

Feeling Moody

Everyone feels moody at some time in their lives. This feeling may cause them to behave in different ways such as isolating themselves from friends, not wanting to talk, being rude or aggressive. It is important to recognise the triggers to our moods so that we can develop strategies to deal with these times and cope with such feelings more effectively.

What are your mood triggers? Record these on the brainstorming sheet below:

I get moody when...

Stop, think and compare! Are your triggers similar to those of your friends? Discuss this in a smaller group and feedback.

Mood Cards

Stop and observe! Look carefully at others around you. What are their triggers? What makes them feel moody?

Complete the mood card for the following people in your life:

My parent/carer gets moody when: ____________________ ____________________ ____________________ ____________________	My brother or sister gets moody when: ____________________ ____________________ ____________________
My friend gets moody when: ____________________ ____________________ ____________________ ____________________	My teacher or form tutor gets moody when: ____________________ ____________________ ____________________
My head teacher gets moody when: ____________________ ____________________ ____________________	My neighbour gets moody when: ____________________ ____________________ ____________________

My (your choice!) gets moody when: ____________________ ____________________ ____________________

Are there any similarities or differences in these triggers? How does each individual feel prior to getting in a mood?

Is there anything that you could do to help each of these individuals? Record your ideas on the reverse of the sheet.

Manage that Mood!
Problem-solve!

Have a go at using this format in order to problem-solve a range of situations or events that might cause you to feel moody. Think carefully about the strategies you might use (anger spoilers, stress management, talking to a friend). Share your solutions and compare them with a friend.

Step 1 **Identify**	Step 2 **Clarify**
This is the situation that causes me to feel moody:	These are the things that I can change in this situation:
Step 3 **Articulate**	Step 4 **Solve it!**
These are the strategies I can use in order to change the situation and the way I respond:	This is exactly what I will try to do:

Take Home Task

Good Moods!

When you're feeling down, moody or just plain fed-up, what will turn your mood around? Try to think of all the things you can do and then complete the following note to yourself:

Dear ____________________

Next time I feel moody or think that I'm getting really fed up with life, I'll aim to help myself cope better by:

1. ______________________________

2. ______________________________

3. ______________________________

4. ______________________________

5. ______________________________

6. ______________________________

7. ______________________________

8. ______________________________

Now – stick this letter in a prominent place in your room and remember to read it and act on it next time you feel moody! Go for it!

Session 18

Feeling Bereaved

Introduction

This session introduces the concepts of bereavement, grief and loss and encourages the students to identify specific feelings and behaviours associated with such experiences. There is an opportunity for the students to identify the main causes of grief and loss and to consider how people may or may not cope with such experiences. The importance of remembering those we have lost and celebrating their lives is also touched upon and the students can consider different ways in which they themselves and those from other cultures may celebrate the lives of others. Finally, the students are asked to devise a message that they would like to give to someone significant in their lives.

The facilitator can elicit the students' definitions of bereavement via a brainstorming approach and record these on a whiteboard or flip-chart. An initial definition can be provided to aid the students' thinking:

Feeling bereaved is when you feel a great deal of pain, grief and loss because you have lost someone or something that you loved or experienced a big change in your life.

Questions for Circle Time

During this part of the session the students can focus upon the following questions:

- When did you last feel sad and why?
- What is the biggest sadness that you have experienced in your life?
- Who helped you to cope with your feelings and how?
- If someone you loved died how would you celebrate their lives?
- If your best friend lost a parent/carer through either illness or a divorce how would you support them? What would you do and say?

Activity 1 – Feeling Bereaved

This activity requires the students to consider the range of feelings that people would experience after having coped with a significant loss in their lives. The facilitator may like to point out that this sense of bereavement does not just attach itself to the death of a loved one but may also be encountered when parents divorce or young people are asked to quickly leave their country and become refugees. It is important to note that feelings of grief and loss can be experienced in a variety of situations and contexts. In this activity the students are asked to work in a small group and record all the feelings that they might experience in such a situation. It may be helpful just to allocate a student to be a scribe. This is a sensitive activity and the facilitator will need to be aware of the students who may be currently experiencing such difficulties. Discretion should be used as to whether or not this is an appropriate session for some such students at this time.

Activity 2 – Causes of Grief and Loss

This activity reinforces the fact that both students and adults experience a range of changes and losses.

The students are required to complete the activity sheet by ticking against any experiences that they may have had or any experiences that members of their families or friends may have had. This is a sensitive activity and the facilitator will need to continually be aware of any students who may find this particularly difficult at this point in time. Finally, this activity requires the students to reflect carefully upon how people may or may not have coped with these experiences and to analyse any similarities or differences in the processes that they may have engaged in during these times.

Activity 3 – Celebrating a Life

The students are asked to consider how they would celebrate the life of someone they had loved and to identify any ceremonies that they may have had. They are asked whether they would create a memory book, write poetry or have a special remembrance day. This activity encourages the students to also focus upon any cultural differences and perhaps to learn more about both themselves and others' responses to the experiences of death and loss.

Take Home Task – Letter to a loved one

This is an extremely personal task and consequently has been nominated as the take home activity for this particular session. The students are asked to think of someone who is really special to them and to imagine what it would be like if they were no longer there for them. The students are asked to consider how they would feel and they are required to write a note to this significant person in order to let them know how much they meant and how much they were valued.

It may be helpful for the facilitator to discuss this activity in a little more detail prior to asking the students to complete it at home. Very often, when someone that we love does die the feelings that we then encounter can very often include guilt and remorse – usually because we neglected to say or do some of the things that we wanted to prior to that person dying. This activity reinforces the importance of communicating with and showing affection, respect and empathy towards those who are significant to us and who show us love in return.

Plenary

The brainstorming approach can be used in order to address the following questions:

- What have we learnt about this particular feeling?
- What have we learnt about how we experience this feeling?
- Have we learnt about how others experience this feeling?
- Are there any new concepts that we have learnt?
- Are there any new skills that we have been able to identify?
- How will this session impact upon us now and in the future?

Feeling Bereaved

When someone suffers a significant loss they will experience a range of feelings. Work in a small group and try to record all the feelings that they might experience.

Causes of Grief and Loss

Both the students and adults will experience changes and losses. Look at the list below. Tick against **A**: any experiences you have had and **B**: any experiences that members of your family or friends may have had.

Change or loss	A	B
Verbal, physical or emotional traumas		
Change of home		
Change of country		
Death of a family member		
Divorce or separation		
Family breakdown		
Friends or family moving away		
Homelessness		
Illness		
Imprisoned family member		
New siblings		
Parent/carer losing job		
Parent/carer returning to work		
Loss of self-esteem		

Stop, think and reflect.

Think carefully about how people may or may not have coped with these experiences. Do you think that they went through a similar process?

Celebrating a Life

How would you celebrate the life of someone you had loved? What ceremonies would you have? Would you create a memory book, write poetry or have a special remembrance day? Record your ideas in the post-it notes.

Compare notes with a friend. What is similar or different in your approach?

Take Home Task

Letter to a Loved One

Think of someone who is really special to you and imagine what it would feel like if they were no longer with you. How would you feel? Write a note to them in order to let them know how much they mean to you.

Dear

Session 19

Feeling Motivated

Introduction

This session reinforces the importance of maintaining a positive outlook and being able to self-motivate oneself. The students are initially asked to identify their own motivation, that is, what motivates them to achieve and succeed in life. They are then encouraged to compare their own motivators with a friend and to analyse any similarities or differences. The notion of locus of control is highlighted as the students are required to analyse whether or not certain successes were due to chance or personal motivation of the characters involved. There is a further opportunity for the students to self-reflect and to identify an ideal self, that is, the person that they would truly like to be in the future. To reach such an ideal and to remain motivated to do so, the students are finally required to identify changes that they may be able to make in order to achieve such a positive outcome for themselves.

The facilitator can elicit the students' definitions as to 'feeling motivated' and record these on a whiteboard or flip-chart. An initial definition can be provided as follows:

Feeling motivated is when you feel that you can achieve and succeed and that you really want to do something positive in your life.

Icebreaker

This icebreaker is entitled 'First Impressions'. The facilitator can ask the students to work in pairs and consider the following questions:

- What do you feel when you walk into school in the morning?
- Name the first feelings that come to mind.
- Why is this?
- Would you like to experience different feelings?
- What would make you feel differently?

The students can work in pairs and then feedback their responses to the group as a whole.

Questions for Circle Time

During this part of the session the students can focus upon the following questions:

- Talk about one thing that you have done really well that you are particularly proud of.
- What was the hardest thing that you had to achieve and why was it so difficult for you?
- What makes you want to do well in your life?
- Have you ever been able to motivate someone else to succeed?
- How did you do this?
- How can we keep ourselves motivated? What do we need to do?
- When have you ever felt de-motivated and what was the cause of this?
- Were you able to get yourself out of this negative situation? If so, how did you do it?

Activity 1 – Mighty Motivators

This is an individual exercise in which each student is required to identify what motivates them to achieve and succeed in life. They are also asked to consider what motivates them to get on with other people and form good relationships with them. These ideas are recorded on a brainstorming chart and the students are then able to compare their motivators with a partner or friend. There is an opportunity for discussion here in which the students can analyse any similarities or differences and consider whether or not our motivations and motivators are particularly person specific.

Activity 2 – Magic or Motivation?

In this activity the students are presented with a range of scenarios. The notion of locus of control and the importance of analysing behaviours and reflecting upon the importance of remaining in control and accepting responsibility for behaviours and outcomes are dealt with. The students are finally encouraged to describe a situation where they were motivated to achieve something. It may be helpful for them to discuss this with a partner and to compare any similarities or differences in their motivations, behaviours and outcomes.

Activity 3 – Hit your Target, Go for the Ideal

This ideal self-activity is influenced by personal construct psychology approaches. The students are required to identify who and what they would ideally like to be. They are asked to draw their ideal self in the picture frame provided on the worksheet and then to identify desired characteristics and achievements around the frame.

Take Home Task – Go for your goals!

This activity leads on directly from Activity 3 as the students are now required to identify three things that they may be able to change now in order to reach their ideal. This is a practical task in that the students are asked to be realistic in identifying things that they can do to help themselves and to also identify how others might be able to help them in this process. Finally, the students are asked to identify how they know when they have achieved their goals, that is, what will be different for them.

Plenary

The brainstorming approach can be used in order to address the following questions:

- What have we learnt about this particular feeling?
- What have we learnt about how we experience this feeling?
- Have we learnt about how others experience this feeling?
- Are there any new concepts that we have learnt?
- Are there any new skills that we have been able to identify?
- How will this session impact upon us now and in the future?

Mighty Motivators

What motivates you to achieve and succeed? What motivates you to get on with others and form rewarding relationships? What motivates you to do your best? Record your ideas on the brainstorming chart.

Compare your motivators with a friend? Are they similar or different? Why do you think this is? Are motivators person specific or are there things that motivate everyone? Record your ideas on the reverse of the sheet.

Magic or Motivation?

Is it luck or were they motivated? Discuss these scenarios in each section below and then feedback your ideas to the group.

NB Think about how each person may have felt and how this might have impacted upon his or her behaviour.

Jason did very well in his maths exam. He felt proud of his result as his teacher had thought he might fail.	Carla lost 16lbs at Weight Watchers. She felt good about herself and knew she wouldn't be teased anymore.
George got into the basketball team. He was determined to do this and practised hard every day.	Teneisha went into her new form and smiled at the other girls. She wanted to make new friends. Two of them smiled back and asked her to sit next to them.
Michael was going to Spain for his holiday. He had saved up for the last 12 months and was sure to have a great time.	Adil found reading difficult. He needed to practise every day and decided to do this because he was worried about his exams.
Matt got into Arsenal's under-18 side. He was pleased but his dad was ecstatic as it had been his lifelong ambition.	Patrick had £16 but needed another £35 to get some new trainers. He decided to get himself a paper round to save up the money.
Ella wanted to win a best attendance award so she made sure that she went into school every day for a term and consequently she was rewarded!	Fergus wanted to see his Dad as he hadn't been able to since his parents divorced. He phoned and left at least 16 messages until his dad called back and invited him over.

Think of a situation where you were motivated to achieve something in particular.

What was your motivation?

Did you achieve your goal?

Hit Your Target! Go for the Ideal!

Who and what would you ideally like to be? Draw your 'ideal self' in the frame below and then identify your desired characteristics and achievements around the frame.

My Ideal Self

Stop and think! How can you move nearer to becoming this kind of person? Use the take home handout to record your goals and identify the strategies and resources that you might need.

Take Home Task

Go for your Goals!

Three things I can change in order to reach my ideal!

1. ____

____

2. ____

____

3. ____

____

Things I can do to help myself achieve this:

Things others can do to help me achieve this:

How will I know when I have achieved my goals? What will be different?

Session 20

Course Review

Introduction

This final session encourages the students to reflect upon the course as a whole and to identify and articulate the skills and strategies that they have learnt. There is also an opportunity for the students to re-visit their initial personal rating scales and to identify and assess their development of skills in each of the key areas as follows:

- an awareness of feelings
- personal insight
- self-assurance
- self-control
- authenticity
- accountability
- flexibility
- self-motivation.

There is an opportunity for the students to formulate specific targets for themselves in each of the key skill areas of Emotional Literacy alongside celebrating the fact that they have successfully completed the course.

In this final session the students can be asked to define the notion of Emotional Literacy and the facilitator can record these personal definitions on the whiteboard or flip-chart and highlight any similarities or differences in the responses provided.

Icebreaker

This icebreaker is entitled 'Feelings Alphabet'. The students are asked to work in small groups and are allocated five minutes in which to formulate a feelings alphabet. They are required to identify one feeling word for each letter of the alphabet, for example, A for anger, B for bereaved, C for carefree, D for dreadful, E for excited. Once again this activity reinforces social skills and the ability to co-operate effectively in a group context.

Questions for Circle Time

During this part of the session the students can focus upon the following questions:

- How would you define Emotional Literacy?
- What key skills do you think you have developed in this course?
- Do you think it is important to be able to effectively manage your feelings?
- How would you describe someone who is emotionally literate?
- What is the feeling that you find most comfortable?
- What is the feeling that you find least comfortable?
- How do you cope with your most uncomfortable feelings?

Activity 1 – My Emotional Survival kit

This activity requires the students to identify the skills and tools that they might need to survive emotionally in life. It also provides an opportunity for them to articulate and record strategies and skills that they have learnt on the emotional survival course. Each student is asked to record his or her thoughts, feelings and ideas on the brainstorming sheet provided. Once these have been completed it may well be helpful for the facilitator to ask for feedback and to record similarities, differences and key skills on the whiteboard or flip-chart. Also, it will be important to encourage the students to discuss their ideas as they work through this sheet in order to prompt thinking and support for one another.

Activity 2 – Emotional Survival Personal Rating Scale

This self-reflection exercise is aimed at encouraging the students to analyse the level of their skills development throughout the course and to provide them with an opportunity to compare their initial ratings with those that they will now make. The idea here is to reinforce the skills learnt and the fact that change is possible for everyone and an important and ongoing process that we will all continue to experience. Once again, the students are asked to rate their own skills using a scale from 0-5. 0=not at all, 3=sometimes and 5=always. It may be helpful to initially discuss the eight key skills and to ensure that the students are in agreement as to the meaning of each.

Once again, the students are asked to identify highest and lowest scores and the strongest and weakest key skills.

Activity 3 – Emotional Literacy Target Sheet

This final self-reflection activity leads on directly from the personal rating scale. The students are asked to rate themselves overall for each of the key skills on a scale of 1-10. They are then asked to work out a personal target for each area in order to further improve their skills.

Take Home Task

This take home task does not require any work on the part of the students! It is simply a Celebration Certificate which can be awarded at the end of the session to each of the students for having successfully completed the emotional survival course.

Plenary

It may be helpful to allocate some additional time to this final plenary session in order for the students to reflect, discuss and analyse the success and enjoyment levels of the emotional survival course as a whole. It may be helpful to utilise the following list of key questions in order to prompt thinking and participation in this final plenary session.

- What have we learnt about our feelings?
- Why is it important for us to deal effectively with our emotions?
- Are there any new concepts or language that we have learnt during this course?
- What are the most helpful skills that we have been able to identify and make use of?
- What difference has this course made to us?
- Will having done this course impact on us in any way in the future?
- What have we enjoyed most about the course and what have we found most useful?
- What would we change about this course if we were to have the opportunity to do so?

My Emotional Survival Kit

What skills and tools do you need in order to survive? What have I learnt on the emotional survival course?

Record your thoughts, feelings and ideas on this brainstorming sheet.

How Are Your Skills?

How is your Emotional Literacy?

How do you rate?

Read each statement and tick against each scale.

0 = not at all   3 = sometimes   5 = always.

Awareness of your feelings

You know what you are feeling.	1	2	3	4	5
You can label your feelings.	1	2	3	4	5
You know when your feelings affect your work.	1	2	3	4	5
You know when your feelings affect your relationships.	1	2	3	4	5

Personal insight

You know your strengths.	1	2	3	4	5
You know your weaknesses.	1	2	3	4	5
You can take constructive criticism from others.	1	2	3	4	5
You don't take yourself too seriously.	1	2	3	4	5
You know when you've done something well and can feel good about yourself.	1	2	3	4	5

Self assurance

You act confidently in most situations.	1	2	3	4	5
You stick up for the things you think are right.	1	2	3	4	5
Other people think you are confident.	1	2	3	4	5

How Are Your Skills?
Continued

Self-control

You can stop yourself when you know you're behaving in a way that will cause problems (for you and others).	1 2 3 4 5
You can keep calm under pressure.	1 2 3 4 5
You can handle uncomfortable feelings and use strategies to reduce stress and anxiety.	1 2 3 4 5

Authenticity

When you say you'll do something you do it.	1 2 3 4 5
You don't say one thing and then do another.	1 2 3 4 5
You can admit your mistakes.	1 2 3 4 5
You can stand up for what you think even if you are in the minority.	1 2 3 4 5

How Are Your Skills?
Continued

Accountability

You can take responsibility for your behaviour or actions.	1 2 3 4 5
You keep your promises.	1 2 3 4 5
You admit it when you've made a mistake.	1 2 3 4 5

Flexibility

You can cope with changes to your day.	1 2 3 4 5
You don't get stressed by change and can go with the flow.	1 2 3 4 5
You like to be creative and think of new ways of doing things.	1 2 3 4 5

Self-motivation

You like to achieve your best.	1 2 3 4 5
You like to get things done.	1 2 3 4 5
You are committed to your relationships.	1 2 3 4 5
You'll keep going even if things get tough.	1 2 3 4 5
You are optimistic and look for opportunities	1 2 3 4 5
before you look for problems.	1 2 3 4 5

Stop and think

What are your highest scores?

Where are your lowest scores?

Which is your best key skill and which is your weakest?

Emotional Literacy Target Sheet

Reflect and assess

Stop and think!

Rate yourself overall for each key skill (at a scale of 1-10).

1 = not at all 5 = sometimes 10 = always

Then try to work out a personal target for each area in order to further improve your skills.

Key Skill	Rating	Personal target
1. Awareness of feelings		•
2. Personal insight		•
3. Self-assurance		•
4. Self- control		•
5. Authenticity		•
6. Accountability		•
7. Flexibility		•
8. Self-motivation		•

Remember! Keep on trying, keep motivated and keep positive!

Go for it!

Celebration Certificate

Well Done!

____

Has successfully participated in the Emotional Survival Course

Signed ______________________ **Date** ______________

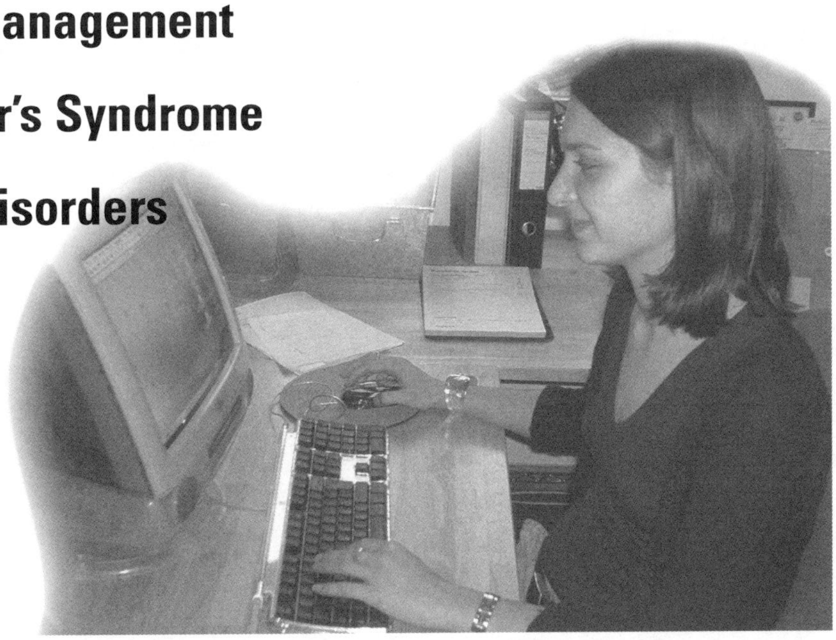